# SpringerBriefs in Intelligent Systems

## Artificial Intelligence, Multiagent Systems, and Cognitive Robotics

This series covers the entire research and application spectrum of intelligent systems, including artificial intelligence, multiagent systems, and cognitive robotics. Typical texts for publication in the series include, but are not limited to, state-of-the-art reviews, tutorials, summaries, introductions, surveys, and in-depth case and application studies of established or emerging fields and topics in the realm of computational intelligent systems. Essays exploring philosophical and societal issues raised by intelligent systems are also very welcome.

Pedro Oliveira · João da Cruz Pereira ·
Paulo Novais

# Architectures for Agentic AI

## Integrating Multi-Agent Systems, Reinforcement Learning, and LLMs for Autonomous Decision-Making

Pedro Oliveira [iD]
ALGORITMI Research Centre/LASI
University of Minho
Braga, Portugal

João da Cruz Pereira [iD]
ALGORITMI Research Centre/LASI
University of Minho
Braga, Portugal

Paulo Novais [iD]
ALGORITMI Research Centre/LASI
University of Minho
Braga, Portugal

ISSN 2196-548X    ISSN 2196-5498  (electronic)
SpringerBriefs in Intelligent Systems
ISBN 978-3-032-24780-3    ISBN 978-3-032-24781-0  (eBook)
https://doi.org/10.1007/978-3-032-24781-0



This Springer imprint is published by the registered company Springer Nature Switzerland AG
The registered company address is: Gewerbestrasse 11, 6330 Cham, Switzerland

If disposing of this product, please recycle the paper.

# Foreword

Generative AI's rapid progress has renewed interest in the notion of agency in artificial intelligence, a concept that has been contemplated by AI for decades. The term "agentic AI" has gained popularity in discussions about generative artificial intelligence, often used to describe autonomous software agents and systems composed of such agents. LLM-based systems that can generate language and plan actions are often described as "agentic agents" and are sometimes presented as marking a qualitative jump in autonomy and reasoning. Yet the foundational literature on intelligent agents articulated these ideas decades ago. The core autonomous agent properties—autonomy, reactivity, proactivity and social ability—remain unchanged, independent of the technological substrate. In this sense, agentic AI reflects continuity with the autonomous-agent/multi-agent system paradigm, albeit amplified by contemporary technologies. By integrating a LLMs, an agent can infer from its perceptions which actions to take to accomplish delegated goals. Systems referred to as Agentic AI implement the classical principles of agency using foundation models. LLM-based agents execute complex tasks through linguistic reasoning, planning and access to external tools. This trend does not constitute a new paradigm but rather a technological expansion of the traditional autonomous agent/multi-agent system framework. Agentive AI does not represent a conceptual break or innovation, but rather a technological evolution of the paradigm of autonomous agents and multi-agent systems. Its relevance lies in its ability to integrate advances in generative AI into pre-existing autonomous agent frameworks. The theoretical continuity between classical agents and LLM-based systems is evidence of the maturity of the field. The current challenge is not to define new types of agents, but to preserve theoretical coherence and avoid conceptual fragmentation. We can see Agentive AI as a stage of neurosymbolic integration that articulates structured knowledge and generative reasoning. Consequently, Agentive AI does not replace autonomous agents/SMA, but rather reinterprets them as ecosystems of linguistic agents, where interaction occurs in natural language and coordination is achieved through mechanisms of argumentation and dialogue. The future of the discipline will depend on the ability to combine the formal tradition of agent theory with new generative and multimodal tools. But we need to align the concepts and frameworks developed over decades with the current state of generative AI, where agents and multi-agent systems based on LLMs have emerged. This book is an important contribution in this regard, representing a significant step forward in how we need to conceive of this new era of multi-agent systems based on generative AI. Agentic AI, Multi-agent Systems (MAS), and Reinforcement Learning (RL) have begun to converge into a class of intelligent behaviour, one that is distributed, communicative and capable of learning from experience. When fused with Large Language Models (LLMs), these paradigms form integrated architectures in which perception, reasoning, learning and communication coexist. Such integration enables systems that adapt as their environments evolve, rather than merely reacting to predefined conditions. When these components are examined individually, the scale of recent progress is already remarkable. Agentic AI now incorporate LLMs as embedded cognitive engines, enabling agents to reason, plan, and communicate in ways increasingly aligned with human interaction. RL has similarly matured, extending beyond classical control problems into domains such as Natural Language Processing (NLP), where it is used to optimise and specialise LLM responses for particular tasks and contexts. These advances, however, reach their full potential only when considered as part of a unified architectural vision, one that this book articulates with clarity and precision. This book arrives at a moment when such a holistic perspective is urgently needed. Rather than presenting Agentic AI as a collection of loosely connected techniques, the authors emphasise the architectural principles that allow autonomy, cooperation and learning to coexist within coherent systems. The discussion moves fluidly between conceptual foundations and applied considerations, highlighting both the opportunities and the constraints that accompany increasingly autonomous intelligence. In doing so, the book resists purely optimistic narratives and instead offers a balanced account of what Agentic AI can realistically achieve, and under what conditions it should be deployed. A notable strength of this work lies in its attention to real-world relevance. By grounding abstract architectures in concrete application scenarios, the book demonstrates how Agentic AI can address complex, dynamic problems in which uncertainty, adaptation and human oversight are central concerns. This practical orientation reinforces the broader message that intelligent systems should not merely be powerful, but also interpretable, responsible and aligned with human objectives. Generally, this book makes a timely and meaningful contribution to the evolving discourse on AI. It will be of interest to researchers, practitioners and advanced students seeking to understand not only the mechanisms behind agentic AI but also their broader implications.

By framing Agentic AI as an integrated and evolving discipline, the authors provide readers with both a conceptual compass and a practical foundation for engaging with the next generation of intelligent systems.

February 2026

Vicent Botti
Valencian Graduate School
and Research Network of Artificial
Intelligence (ValgrAI)
Valencian Research Institute for
Artificial Intelligence (VRAIN)
Universitat Politècnica de València
(UPV)
Valencia, Spain

# Preface

The trajectory of Artificial Intelligence (AI) has been marked by a fundamental transition, moving from purely reactive systems to entities capable of deliberation and autonomous action in highly complex environments. This book, entitled *Architectures for Agentic AI*, emerges at a time when the convergence between Multi-agent Systems (MAS), Reinforcement Learning (RL) and Large Language Models (LLMs) establishes a new paradigm of technological agency. Our purpose with this book is to provide a theoretical and practical basis for understanding this evolution, not as a set of isolated advances, but as a synergistic integration necessary for the creation of intelligent systems that operate with purpose and discernment.

Throughout these pages, we explore the idea that Agentic AI emerges from the intersection of three pillars that define contemporary computational intelligence. We begin by analysing how MAS provide the essential structure for coordination and cooperation, enabling distributed, collaborative intelligence. To this infrastructure, we combine the dynamism of RL, which endows agents with the ability to optimise their behaviour through experience, and the semantic depth of LLMs, which function as cognitive engines capable of reasoning, task decomposition and communication in natural language. This triad not only expands the technical capabilities of the systems but also redefines how humans interact with artificial autonomy.

One of the central themes that runs throughout this work is the imperative of interpretability. For agentic systems to be responsibly integrated into society, their decisions must be transparent and justifiable. We therefore discuss how new architectures can use natural language processing not only for task execution but as a transparent interface that translates opaque computational processes into explanations understandable to the user. This ethical and technical dimension allows the building of a relationship of trust between man and machine, ensuring that autonomy never overrides supervision and human dignity.

To support the theoretical discussions presented here, we include a detailed case study of ecological monitoring in Azorean lakes. This practical example demonstrates how Agentic AI can be applied to solving real-world problems, protecting sensitive ecosystems and supporting decision-making in contexts of environmental uncertainty. By transposing abstract concepts to a natural preservation scenario, we aim to illustrate the transformative potential of these technologies when geared towards the common good and the sustainability of the planet.

This book was written for researchers, software engineering professionals and students who wish to position themselves at the forefront of Artificial Intelligence. We hope this reading offers not only a technical overview of agentic architectures but also a reflection on the responsibilities that accompany the development of autonomous systems. We conclude with the conviction that we are only at the beginning of a new era of collaboration between humans and intelligent agents, a symbiosis where computational capacity unites with ethical deliberation to face the most pressing challenges of our time.

Braga, Portugal

Pedro Oliveira
João da Cruz Pereira
Paulo Novais

**Acknowledgements** The authors wanted to express their deepest gratitude towards all the people who supported them in writing this book. A very special appreciation goes to Dr. Alexandru Ciolan and his team for their help, valuable feedback and expertise. Moreover, appreciation is due to Prof. Vicent Botti for his expertise in the field, being the focus of this book, and for his valuable suggestions and assistance. In addition, we would like to thank our colleagues for providing valuable insights and brainstorming sessions during the conception of this book's ideas and writing path. A special thanks goes to the research centres, namely LASI/ALGORITMI Centre, for providing the necessary support and infrastructure for the book's inception. We are also deeply grateful for the support of our family and friends, whose love, dedication and patience gave us the strength to conceive the book. Without all of them, this book wouldn't have been possible.

The warmth of your encouragement has been the quiet engine behind this achievement.

This work is financed by National Funds through the Portuguese funding agency, FCT—Fundação para a Ciência e a Tecnologia within project 2022.06822.PTDC (https://doi.org/10.54499/2022.06822.PTDC). The work of Pedro Oliveira was supported by the doctoral Grant PRT/BD/154311/2022 financed by the Portuguese Foundation for Science and Technology (FCT), and with funds from European Union, under MIT Portugal Program. The work of Paulo Novais was developed during his sabbatical academic year, specifically in 2025/2026.

**Competing Interests** The authors have no competing interests to declare that are relevant to the content of this manuscript.

# Contents

# Acronyms

| | |
|---|---|
| AI | Artificial Intelligence |
| API | Application Programming Interface |
| BDI | Belief–Desire–Intention |
| CRISP-DM | Cross-Industry Standard Process for Data Mining |
| DL | Deep Learning |
| GPU | Graphical Processing Unit |
| GRPO | Group Relative Policy Optimisation |
| LIME | Local Interpretable Model-agnostic Explanations |
| LLM | Large Language Models |
| MARL | Multi-agent Reinforcement Learning |
| MAS | Multi-agent Systems |
| ML | Machine Learning |
| MLP | Multi-Layer Perceptron |
| MRKL | Modular Reasoning, Knowledge and Language |
| NLP | Natural Language Processing |
| OODA | Observe, Orient, Decide, Act |
| PPO | Proximal Policy Optimisation |
| RL | Reinforcement Learning |
| SHAP | SHapley Additive exPlanations |
| XAI | Explainable Artificial Intelligence |

# Chapter 1
# From Classical AI to Agentic Intelligence

**Abstract** This chapter introduces the conceptual motivation behind Agentic Artificial Intelligence (AI) by tracing the historical evolution of AI paradigms, from rule-based systems to data-driven machine learning and multi-agent approaches. It highlights the limitations of classical AI systems in addressing complex, open-ended, and dynamic real-world problems, particularly those requiring long-term autonomy, contextual reasoning, and adaptive decision-making. By framing intelligence as an emergent, situated, and goal-directed process, the chapter establishes agentivity as a central organising principle. The discussion situates Agentic AI as a response to the growing need for systems capable of integrating perception, learning, reasoning, and interaction over extended time horizons. It concludes by outlining the book's structure and positioning Agentic AI as a unifying paradigm that bridges symbolic reasoning, learning-based methods, and autonomous multi-agent coordination.

## 1.1 The Evolution of AI

A sequence of waves of enthusiasm, disillusionment, and reinvention marks the history of AI. Since its origins in the mid-20th century, AI has oscillated between symbolic, connectionist, and statistical approaches, reflecting attempts to capture, through different avenues, what is understood as 'intelligence' in artificial systems. This evolution is not only technical but also epistemological, as it continually redefines the very concept of reasoning and autonomy in machines [1].

The founding period of AI, in the 1950s and 1960s, was dominated by the symbolic perspective. Researchers such as John McCarthy, Marvin Minsky, Allen Newell, and Herbert Simon sought to formalise human intelligence through logical representations and explicit rules. The central idea was that thought could be reduced to symbolic manipulations performed by a computer, a symbol-processing machine capable of performing deductive reasoning [2]. This gave rise to rule-based systems, problem-solving programs, and the first automatic planning systems.

This approach gave rise to the so-called Classical AI paradigm, which conceived of intelligence as a process of symbolic inference about a well-defined world. The environment was often static, problems were formulated as logical puzzles, and



P. Oliveira et al., *Architectures for Agentic AI*, SpringerBriefs in Intelligent Systems,
https://doi.org/10.1007/978-3-032-24781-0_1

agents acted according to predetermined plans. While these systems were successful in narrow domains, such as board games or rule-based diagnostics, they proved fragile in the face of real-world uncertainty, ambiguity, and complexity [3].

In the 1980s, dissatisfaction with the limitations of symbolic reasoning fueled the renaissance of artificial neural networks, inspired by the brain's biological structure. Connectionism introduced an alternative vision: intelligence could emerge from distributed interactions between simple processing units. This paradigm emphasised learning from data, dynamic adaptation, and generalisation, in contrast to the rigidity of symbolic rules. However, the networks of the time faced computational and theoretical constraints that prevented significant progress until the turn of the millennium [4].

With the explosion of computing power and the massive availability of digital data, AI entered the era of Machine Learning (ML). Statistical algorithms and optimisation methods began to play a central role in pattern extraction and predictions. The introduction of Deep Learning (DL) revitalised connectionism, leading to remarkable achievements in image recognition, machine translation, and Natural Language Processing (NLP) [5]. However, this phase also revealed a paradox: although deep networks exhibit impressive capabilities, their 'intelligence' remains essentially reactive and unintentional. They are systems that recognise patterns but do not act autonomously to pursue their own goals.

The maturity of contemporary AI has generated a new demand: the ability to act autonomously in a dynamic environment, to learn, negotiate, and collaborate with other agents, human or artificial. This transition marks the birth of Agentic AI, which combines symbolic reasoning, statistical learning, and goal-oriented decision-making mechanisms. If classical AI sought to simulate thought and modern AI seeks to imitate perception, Agentic AI seeks to embody action, endowing systems with a sense of agency, that is, the ability to make decisions and adapt to context and values [6].

The trajectory of AI is a movement of increasing autonomy and integration. From explicit rules to distributed learning and, more recently, to coordination among agents, the field has evolved from a model of isolated processing to one of cognitive ecosystems. Today, the frontier of research is less focused on how systems 'think' and more on how they interact, learn, and cooperate. This epistemological shift paves the way for the following discussion: what does it ultimately mean to speak of 'Agentic AI', and why does it represent a new paradigm in the design of intelligent architectures?

## 1.2  The Rise of Agentic AI

The emergence of Agentic AI represents one of the most significant moments in the conceptual and technological evolution of AI. More than an incremental advance, it represents a paradigm shift, shifting the focus from perception and prediction to autonomous, deliberative, and contextual action. In this new phase, AI ceases to be merely an analytical tool and becomes an active actor in complex ecosystems, capable of observing, deciding, learning, and interacting with other human and artificial agents.

For decades, AI was seen primarily as an instrument of intelligent automation, systems designed to perform specific tasks efficiently. The primary goal was to replace or augment human performance in well-defined contexts: diagnosing diseases, predicting failures, and recognising visual or linguistic patterns. However, these systems operated essentially reactively: they received data, processed it, produced results, and awaited new inputs.

Agentivity, by contrast, introduces a qualitative leap. An intelligent agent not only reacts to stimuli but also acts proactively in line with goals, beliefs, and plans. It interprets the environment, formulates hypotheses, adjusts its behaviour, and communicates with other agents to achieve common or individual goals [7]. This ability to act with intention is at the heart of the transition from automatic to autonomous systems.

The rise of Agentic AI results from the convergence of three historical lines of research: Multi-Agent Systems (MAS), Reinforcement Learning (RL), and Large Language Models (LLMs). Each of these traditions contributes an essential pillar to the emergence of computational autonomy.

1. MAS: Since the 1990s, MAS have provided a conceptual framework for modelling societies of agents interacting in shared environments. In these systems, the emphasis is on cooperation, negotiation, and coordination among entities with potentially distinct goals [8]. Game theory, distributed logic, and inter-agent communication protocols form the theoretical foundation of this domain.
2. RL: This paradigm introduced an approach centred on experience and reward optimisation. An agent learns to act by observing the consequences of its actions, adjusting its behaviour policy to maximise the accumulated return over time [9]. This idea of interactive learning has transformed how AI handles dynamic, uncertain environments.
3. LLMs: With the advent of LLMs, such as GPT and other generative language models, the ability to reason symbolically about text, understand complex instructions, and generate contextually coherent responses emerged [10]. More than just linguistic tools, these models now serve as cognitive interfaces, integrating perception, planning, and communication.

The integration of these three strands forms the basis of modern Agentic AI: agents that learn adaptively, communicate naturally, and coordinate with other agents, guided by dynamic goals and principles of autonomous decision-making.

The concept of Agentic AI transcends the simple notion of technical autonomy. It implies the existence of functional intentionality, a form of operational will that guides the system's decisions based on explicit or emergent objectives. An Agentic agent must be able to answer the following questions:

- What do we intend to achieve in this context?
- What actions maximise the probability of success?
- What effects will my decisions have on other agents and the environment?

These questions require capabilities of symbolic representation, adaptive learning, and strategic deliberation, integrated into a single architectural framework. Agentic AI thus emerges as a synthesis of symbolic reasoning, connectionist learning, and autonomous planning. It does not replace previous approaches, but reconfigures them under a new logic of situated and coordinated action [6].

One of the most notable milestones in the rise of Agentic AI is the transition from isolated systems to distributed cognitive ecosystems. Instead of a single centralised model that attempts to solve all problems, we observe the formation of collectives of agents that collaborate, compete, and co-evolve. This vision was inspired by both biology (ant colonies, swarms, ecosystems) and social sciences (organisations, social networks, markets) [7].

Such agent ecosystems are being explored in multiple domains: from cooperative recommendation systems and social simulations to natural resource management, logistics planning, and decentralised digital governance. The challenge becomes designing scalable Agentic architectures capable of handling interdependence, conflict, and uncertainty while maintaining global coherence.

LLMs have introduced a new dimension to Agentic AI: semantic coordination. LLMs serve as cognitive orchestration engines, enabling disparate agents to communicate in an interpretable, context-sensitive manner. In modern Agentic architectures, a LLM can serve as:

- Cognitive interface between human and artificial agents;
- Shared reasoning mechanism, translating abstract goals into concrete plans;
- Context management, synthesising scattered information into coherent representations.

This integration transforms LLMs into "higher-level agents" that supervise, instruct, and evaluate other agents, creating hierarchical decision-making structures [10]. Together with RL and multi-agent theory, they enable the construction of reflective and socially responsive systems.

The rise of Agentic AI redefines the very relationship between humans and machines. If traditional AI was essentially a computational tool, Agentic AI approaches the role of a cognitive partner, an employee who actively participates in the discovery, analysis, and decision-making process. Rather than replacing humans, Agentic AI tends to complement them, expanding the scope of perception and collective deliberation [11].

This partnership raises new ethical and epistemological questions:

- How can we ensure that agent autonomy does not compromise human oversight?
- What ethical alignment mechanisms should be incorporated into Agentic architectures?

- How can we ensure transparency, accountability, and trust in distributed decision-making ecosystems?

The answers to these questions will be crucial for the future of AI and for how human societies will interact with systems endowed with increasing cognitive autonomy.

In short, the rise of Agentic AI represents the shift from perception AI to action AI; from isolated analysis to coordinated interaction; from deterministic calculation to adaptive behaviour. The integration of agents, RL, and linguistic models creates the foundation for a new generation of reflective, proactive, and interconnected systems capable of operating self-sufficiently in complex environments.

## 1.3  What Defines Agentic AI

Agentic AI represents a mature synthesis of decades of research in computational autonomy, distributed cognition, and adaptive learning. Although the term 'Agentic' has been widely popularised in technical and media contexts, its formal definition remains under construction. Understanding what defines Agentic AI involves distinguishing between systems that merely execute instructions and those that deliberate and act in accordance with their own goals, dynamically adjusting to the environment and to social interactions.

Not every autonomous system is Agentic. Technical autonomy, that is, the ability to function without direct human intervention, is insufficient to characterise Agentic systems. Many automated systems, such as temperature controllers, programmed vehicles, or negotiation algorithms, operate independently, yet lack any intentional representation of their actions or goals

Cognitive agents, in turn, presupposes that the system understands, even if only operationally, the purpose and context of its actions [12]. This understanding manifests through mechanisms of deliberation, consequence prediction, and strategic adaptation. An Agentic agent 'knows' not only what to do, but also why it does it and how it should alter its behaviour when the environment changes.

Conceptually, Agentic AI can be described as a system that integrates four fundamental dimensions: perception, deliberation, learning, and action. These dimensions interact cyclically and interdependently, forming the core of the Agentic architecture.

1. **Contextual Perception** Agentic perception goes beyond simply receiving data. It involves the semantic interpretation of the environment and the construction of internal models that allow the agent to situate itself in space and time [6]. An Agentic agent must be able to perceive not only what is happening, but also what it means for its goals.

2. **Intentional Deliberation** Deliberation is the process by which the agent formulates hypotheses, evaluates alternatives, and chooses courses of action based on explicit goals. Unlike a purely statistical response, deliberation involves symbolic reasoning and the evaluation of consequences. In contemporary systems,

this function is often supported by LLMs integrated with planning modules and hybrid symbolic reasoning models [13].

3. **Adaptive Learning** RL and other forms of ML enable agents to continuously adapt to environmental conditions. Adaptive learning is the mechanism that confers behavioural plasticity, that is, the ability to change strategies based on accumulated experience. The combination of supervised, unsupervised, and RL generates agents with varying degrees of epistemic autonomy [9].

4. **Autonomous and Socially Sensitive Action** Finally, action is the convergence point of perception, deliberation, and learning. In the Agentic context, acting implies evaluating the social and environmental impact of decisions. Agentic agents must possess mechanisms for ethical alignment and social cooperation, mainly when operating in multi-agent ecosystems. Action ceases to be purely instrumental and becomes relational and contextualised [7].

These four pillars are articulated in a cyclical architecture of observation–decision–learning–action, similar to the Observe, Orient, Decide, Act (OODA) loop model, but enriched with semantic and social capabilities.

Recent literature proposes different models to formalise Agentic AI. Among the most influential are the BDI (Belief-Desire-Intention) architectures and their hybrid extensions [14].

- Beliefs represent the agent's knowledge of the world.
- Desires express the goals or desired future states.
- Intentions reflect the agent's plans and commitments.

Modern Agentic AI extends this framework by incorporating continuous learning, probabilistic reasoning, and generative linguistic models, enabling a more fluid integration of symbolism and empiricism. LLM-driven BDI architectures thus emerge as hybrid forms in which LLMs provide contextual reasoning and natural communication, while RL and planning modules ensure action execution and optimisation [15].

Three complementary concepts help clarify what distinguishes Agentic AI: autonomy, reflexivity, and accountability.

- Autonomy refers to the ability to define and execute plans without constant supervision. However, pure autonomy can be dangerous if not accompanied by mechanisms for ethical alignment and contextual validation [16].
- Reflexivity implies the agent's ability to monitor and adjust its own cognitive processes. It is a form of artificial metacognition, in which the system 'observes' itself and modifies its behaviour based on internal performance or coherence metrics [16].
- Responsibility emerges when the agent is designed to recognise the implications of its decisions on social or ecological systems. This is where the concept of agency intersects with AI ethics and AI alignment [17].

**Table 1.1**  Comparison between conventional AI and agentic AI

| Dimension | Conventional AI | Agentic AI |
| --- | --- | --- |
| Primary objective | Execute predefined tasks with fixed goals | Achieve dynamic objectives in open and evolving contexts |
| Type of autonomy | Technical autonomy (data-driven reactions) | Cognitive autonomy (deliberation and adaptation) |
| Knowledge source | Data models and statistical patterns | Experience, dialogue, and symbolic reasoning |
| Interaction mode | Limited and unidirectional | Collaborative, multi-agent, and context-aware |
| Learning paradigm | Supervised or pre-trained learning | Continuous, exploratory, and goal-oriented learning |
| Ethical capacity | Absent or implicit | Embedded and deliberative ethical alignment |
| Communication modality | Programmatic or API-based exchanges | Linguistic and interpretative communication (via LLMs) |

The integration of these three principles transforms the agent from a mere policy executor into an active participant in a normative ecosystem (Table 1.1).  One way to understand the specificity of Agentic AI is to compare it to conventional AI:

This comparison shows that Agentic AI does not replace conventional AI but rather expands and contextualises it. Its value lies in its ability to deal with uncertainty, negotiate meaning, and integrate social and ethical dimensions into the decision-making process.

More than a technical advancement, Agentic AI constitutes a new episteme for AI, a different way of understanding what it means to 'be intelligent'. Intelligence ceases to be merely the ability to solve problems and becomes the ability to actively participate in a shared world, generating meaning, predictions, and actions consistent with values and goals. Agentic AI thus proposes a redefinition of the very concept of intelligence: not as calculation, but as meaningful interaction [11].

This paradigm shift opens the door to a fundamental discussion: if Agentic agents need dynamic, cooperative, and socially relevant contexts, then they also need appropriate architectures that support this complexity. This is precisely the question addressed in the following section.

## 1.4  The Need for Agentic Architectures

The consolidation of Agentic AI reveals a demand that goes beyond mere algorithmic improvement: the need to rethink the very architectures that underpin artificial cognition. The shift from reactive to deliberative intelligence entails an ontological leap that can be achieved only through a structural reorganisation of intelligent systems. Classical AI, built on monolithic, deterministic foundations, has proven insufficient to handle open, uncertain, and socially complex environments. What is at stake is not just a question of performance, but of epistemological coherence: architecture defines how a system thinks, learns, and acts, and therefore determines the limits of its Agentic AI [7].

Traditional AI architectures were designed for predictable contexts, where knowledge is stable, and objectives are defined a priori. In these structures, symbolic reasoning and statistical learning operate in isolated modules, communicating in a limited and often linear manner [2]. The result is a form of instrumental intelligence, capable of solving well-defined problems but unable to adapt to emerging situations or negotiate meaning in dynamic environments. The lack of integration between perception, deliberation, and action creates a gap between what the system understands and what it actually does. This disjunction is incompatible with the notion of Agentic AI, which requires a unified and self-regulating cognitive cycle [6].

For intelligence to become truly Agentic, it is necessary to design systems in which the perception of the world, the formulation of intentions, and the execution of actions form a continuous cycle of interpretation and readjustment. This principle implies abandoning the architectural rigidity of classical AI in favour of a modular, adaptive structure in which each component contributes to the overall cognitive process without losing its functional autonomy. Modularity, in this context, is not just an engineering choice but an epistemological imperative: it allows the system to reorganise its internal priorities, reevaluate objectives, and redistribute cognitive resources in response to context. Intelligence thus becomes an emergent phenomenon, a product of the dynamic interaction between specialised subsystems and the external environment.

The need for Agentic architectures also stems from the growing interdependence between multiple artificial and human agents. In the real world, decision-making rarely occurs in isolation. Intelligent systems are called upon to cooperate, compete, and negotiate in complex ecosystems, such as information networks, digital platforms, and urban or natural environments. In this framework, MAS theory serves as the conceptual basis for structuring interactions among distinct cognitive entities. From this perspective, an agent is not simply an autonomous unit but a participant in an artificial social network that shares information, coordinates strategies, and influences collective behaviour. This relational dimension is essential to understanding contemporary agency, which is defined less by individuality and more by the capacity for coordinated participation [12].

However, interaction alone is not enough. For agents to act effectively and adaptively, they must possess mechanisms for experiential learning. This is where RL takes on a structuring role. Unlike supervised learning, which relies on labelled data and static contexts, RL is based on the continuous interaction between the agent and the environment. Each action generates a consequence that feeds back into the decision-making process, enabling the development of behavioural policies tailored to experience. When this learning is extended to multiple agents, so-called Multi-Agent Reinforcement Learning (MARL), collective properties of coordination, negotiation, and cooperation emerge. Rewards cease to be individual and become dependent on harmony among agents, establishing a rudimentary form of operational ethics. RL, therefore, provides the adaptive backbone of Agentic architectures, giving them plasticity and the capacity for self-transformation [18].

The third dimension that completes this picture is language. The emergence of LLMs has redefined the interface between artificial cognition and the symbolic world. These models not only process text but also operate as semantic mediators between different levels of reasoning. Their integration into Agentic architectures introduces a new layer of cognitive cohesion: through language, agents can describe states, justify decisions, and negotiate intentions. The LLM therefore functions as an interpretive infrastructure that unifies distributed thinking, enabling heterogeneous systems to communicate in an intelligible, contextually relevant manner. In a sense, the LLM is the semantic fabric that connects the sensory and deliberative components, functioning as a kind of 'linguistic cortex' of AI [10].

The conjunction of MAS, RL, and LLMs forms an integrated intelligence through the ability to communicate, learn, and interpret. MAS ensure the social dimension of intelligence, RL ensures continuous adaptation, and language models introduce the capacity for communication and symbolic reasoning. When integrated, these three axes produce a system endowed with cognitive autonomy and context sensitivity. The result is a non-hierarchical, yet ecological, architecture in which intelligence emerges from the interactions, both internal and external, that the system maintains with the world. This model is closer to a cognitive ecosystem than a traditional machine: a space where flows of information, learning, and communication intertwine continuously and recursively.

However, this integration poses new challenges of scalability and coherence. As the number of agents and the volume of interactions increase, the risk of cognitive fragmentation and information collapse also increases. Maintaining consistency in a distributed system requires mechanisms of governance, coordination, and trust. Contemporary Agentic AI seeks to resolve this tension through flexible hierarchical forms, in which specialised agents operate under the supervision of cognitive coordinators, often LLMs trained to synthesise information and harmonise objectives. This is a structure of collective deliberation, inspired by both biological organisms and social systems, which transforms AI into a space for dialogue and co-evolution [13].

The need for Agentic architectures ultimately signals a more profound movement in the very concept of intelligence. It is no longer enough to process data or predict results; it is necessary to understand contexts, assign meanings, and act with discernment. An Agentic architecture must support this new form of distributed rationality, in which knowledge is shared, action is situated, and learning is ongoing. Its purpose is not to replace humans but to expand the horizon of collective cognition. By integrating perception, deliberation, communication, and learning into a single reflective circuit, Agentic architectures lay the foundation for truly autonomous and relational intelligence. They are, therefore, more than a technological advance: they constitute a new grammar of intelligent action [6].

## 1.5   Book Structure

The structure of this book was designed to reflect the evolutionary movement of Agentic AI itself: from conceptual foundations to applied practice, from theoretical abstraction to experimental realisation. The narrative path that follows is guided by the idea that Agentic AI is not merely a technical property, but a new cognitive paradigm that integrates perception, deliberation, and learning into a coherent framework of artificial autonomy. Each chapter corresponds to a layer of this journey, progressively deepening the principles and mechanisms that underpin Architectures for Agentic AI.

This chapter establishes the historical and epistemological framework of the work. Drawing on the genealogy of AI, from classical symbolic approaches to the emergence of distributed cognition, the book demonstrates the inevitability of Agentic architectures. This introduction argues that contemporary AI requires a structural overhaul to integrate reasoning, learning, and communication within cooperative cognitive ecosystems.

Chapter 2 constitutes the theoretical foundation of the book. It examines the conceptual foundations of Agentic AI, beginning with MAS, which evolves into agents, culminating in Agentic AI. LLMs are addressed, exploring their role as cognitive mediators and semantic interpreters within these architectures. This chapter, therefore, serves as a bridge between the theoretical tradition of distributed AI and the contemporary formulation of Agentic intelligence.

Chapter 3 moves from the conceptual to the architectural level. It discusses the design principles that guide the construction of Agentic systems, including the agent's environments, agent typologies, communication and cooperation modalities, and orchestration layers that ensure coherence and operational robustness. This chapter details the forms of coordination between agents, both horizontally (peer-to-peer cooperation) and vertically (supervision and hierarchical control).

Chapter 4 introduces one of the most crucial dimensions of contemporary AI: interpretability. If artificial autonomy is to coexist with human trust, then agent decisions must be understandable and justifiable. This chapter examines the foundations of interpretability in AI, moving from traditional algorithmic explanation techniques to NLP-based approaches. Next, we demonstrate how LLMs have become instruments of cognitive transparency, capable of generating coherent textual descriptions of the internal reasoning of Agentic agents.

Chapter 5 dives deeper into the domain of dynamic learning, with an emphasis on the role of reinforcement learning within Agentic architectures. This chapter describes the theoretical foundations of RL, its integration into multi-agent systems, and how this integration enhances adaptive cooperation and continuous optimisation. We also explore the use of RL in fine-tuning linguistic models, allowing them to adapt to specific domains and produce contextually relevant responses.

Chapter 6 focuses solely on the practical application, introducing the case study of an Azorean lake as a concrete field of application that demonstrates how Agentic AI can take an active role in ecological monitoring and management. The case thus serves as an experimental thread that will run throughout the book, connecting theory and practice throughout the following chapters. It examines the conceptual integration of these dimensions, mapping the Agentic principles, autonomy, communication, adaptability, and reflexivity. Thereby, the presentation of the architectural implementation of the case study demonstrates how the concepts of Agentic AI materialise in an ecological decision system that integrates agents of perception, deliberation, and semantic coordination. In addition, for interpretability purposes, the seamless application of LLMs via the Agentic architecture demonstrates how it can translate environmental analysis into interpretable narratives understandable to experts and human decision-makers. Finally, the LLM is then fine-tuned using RL not only as an optimisation technique but also as a domain-specific adaptation, keeping in line with coherent ethical considerations.

Chapter 7 concludes the book by revisiting the theoretical and practical threads that structure it. It begins with a summary of the main contributions, highlighting the connection between the principles of Agentic AI and the proposed architectural solutions. This is followed by a reflection on lessons learned from translating theory into practice, highlighting the tensions between conceptual abstraction and experimental implementation. This chapter also discusses the broader impact of Agentic architectures, both scientifically and ethically, recognising that artificial autonomy requires new frameworks of accountability, interpretability, and trust. Finally, future research directions are outlined, pointing to a horizon where Agentic AI consolidates itself as the bridge between intelligent systems and meaningful human interaction. The book, therefore, concludes with a reflection on the transformative potential of this new paradigm, which promises to redefine the relationships among technology, knowledge, and action.

The relationship between the chapters is deliberately progressive and cumulative. Each part sets the stage for the next, building an arc of conceptual coherence that stretches from the historical understanding of AI to its contemporary Agentic expression. The case study, introduced in the first chapter, serves as a cross-cutting axis, providing empirical context for testing the theoretical hypotheses and demonstrating the practical applicability of the ideas presented. Through this alternation between theory and practice, the book proposes an integrated approach: understanding Agentic AI not simply as a technical evolution, but as a philosophical reconfiguration of the very notion of intelligence. Thus, the journey that begins with a description of the origins of AI and culminates with a reflection on its ethical and societal impact mirrors the path of the discipline. This path leads from machine to agent, from calculation to deliberation, and from prediction to understanding.

# References


1. Baoyu Liang, Yuchen Wang, and Chao Tong. "AI Reasoning in Deep Learning Era: From Symbolic AI to Neural–Symbolic AI". In: *Mathematics* 13.11 (2025). ISSN: 2227-7390. DOI: https://doi.org/10.3390/math13111707. URL: https://www.mdpi.com/2227-7390/13/11/1707.

2. Dimitrios Angelis, Filippos Sofos, and Theodoros E Karakasidis. "Artificial intelligence in physical sciences: Symbolic regression trends and perspectives". In: *Archives of Computational Methods in Engineering* (2023), p. 1. DOI: https://doi.org/10.1007/s11831-023-09922-z.

3. Yongjun Xu et al. "Artificial intelligence: A powerful paradigm for scientific research". In: *The Innovation* 2.4 (2021). DOI: https://doi.org/10.1016/j.xinn.2021.100179.

4. Ken Kahn and Niall Winters. "Constructionism and AI: A history and possible futures". In: *British Journal of Educational Technology* 52.3 (2021), pp. 1130–1142. DOI: https://doi.org/10.1111/bjet.13088.

5. Juergen Schmidhuber. "Annotated history of modern ai and deep learning". In: *arXiv preprint* arXiv:2212.11279 (2022). DOI: https://doi.org/10.48550/arXiv.2212.11279.

6. Ken Huang. *Agentic AI*. Springer, 2025. DOI: https://doi.org/10.1007/978-3-031-90026-6.

7. Deepak Bhaskar Acharya, Karthigeyan Kuppan, and B. Divya. "Agentic AI: Autonomous Intelligence for Complex Goals–A Comprehensive Survey". In: *IEEE Access* 13 (2025), pp. 18912–18936. DOI: https://doi.org/10.1109/ACCESS.2025.3532853.

8. Abdollah Amirkhani and Amir Hossein Barshooi. "Consensus in multi-agent systems: a review". In: *Artificial Intelligence Review* 55.5 (2022), pp. 3897–3935. DOI: https://doi.org/10.1007/s10462-021-10097-x.

9. Yutaka Matsuo et al. "Deep learning, reinforcement learning, and world models". In: *Neural Networks* 152 (2022), pp. 267–275. DOI: https://doi.org/10.1016/j.neunet.2022.03.037.

10. Wayne Xin Zhao et al. "A survey of large language models". In: *arXiv preprint* arXiv:2303.18223 1.2 (2023). DOI: https://doi.org/10.1145/3744746.

11. Ajay Bandi et al. "The Rise of Agentic AI: A Review of Definitions, Frameworks, Architectures, Applications, Evaluation Metrics, and Challenges". In: *Future Internet* 17.9 (2025). ISSN: 1999-5903. DOI: https://doi.org/10.3390/fi17090404.

12. Juan Mendoza-Collazos and Jordan Zlatev. "A cognitive-semiotic approach to agency: Assessing ideas from cognitive science and neuroscience". In: *Biosemiotics* 15.1 (2022), pp. 141–170. DOI: https://doi.org/10.1007/s12304-022-09473-z.

13. Jason W Burton et al. "How large language models can reshape collective intelligence". In: *Nature human behaviour* 8.9 (2024), pp. 1643–1655. DOI: https://doi.org/10.1038/s41562-024-01959-9.

14. Rafael C Cardoso and Angelo Ferrando. "A review of agent-based programming for multi-agent systems". In: *Computers* 10.2 (2021), p. 16. DOI: https://doi.org/10.3390/computers10020016.

15. V. Botti. *Agentic AI and Multiagentic: Are We Reinventing the Wheel?*. 2025. arXiv: 2506.01463 [cs.MA]. URL: https://arxiv.org/abs/2506.01463.

16. Yannis Ktenas. "Autonomy and Reflexivity: On the significance and limitations of Castoriadis's concept of an autonomous society". In: *International Journal of Social Imaginaries* 3.2 (2024), pp. 196–214. DOI: https://doi.org/10.1163/27727866-bja00043.

17. Christel Baier, Florian Funke, and Rupak Majumdar. *A Game-Theoretic Account of Responsibility Allocation*. 2021. DOI: https://doi.org/10.48550/arXiv.2105.09129. arXiv: 2105.09129 [cs.GT].

18. Lorenzo Canese et al. "Multi-agent reinforcement learning: A review of challenges and applications". In: *Applied Sciences* 11.11 (2021), p. 4948. DOI: https://doi.org/10.3390/app11114948.

# Chapter 2
# Theoretical Foundations of Agentic AI

**Abstract** This chapter develops the theoretical foundations underlying Agentic Artificial Intelligence (AI) by examining the integration of Multi-Agent Systems (MAS), Reinforcement Learning (RL), and language-based reasoning. Multi-agent frameworks are reviewed to establish the principles of decentralised control, interaction, and emergent behaviour. The chapter then extends these foundations by incorporating learning dynamics that enable agents to adapt policies through experience and interaction. A central contribution of this chapter is the examination of communication and coordination mechanisms, with particular emphasis on the role of language as a shared semantic substrate for reasoning and collaboration. By formalising how agents can combine learning, communication, and deliberation, the chapter distinguishes Agentic AI from traditional MAS. The discussion highlights how agentic systems support long-horizon objectives, dynamic goal management, and reflective decision-making, thereby enabling persistent autonomy in complex environments.

## 2.1 Multi-agent Systems

MAS represent a fundamental paradigm in AI and distributed computing in which multiple autonomous entities, referred to as agents, coexist and interact within a shared environment [1]. Each agent can perceive its surroundings, make decisions based on internal objectives, and perform actions that affect both the environment and other agents. Unlike centralised or monolithic software systems, where intelligence and control are concentrated in a single component, MAS are inherently decentralised, allowing intelligence to emerge from local interactions rather than from global coordination. This decentralised nature makes MAS particularly well-suited for complex, dynamic, and large-scale systems where adaptability, robustness, and scalability are critical, which is perfectly suited to our world, where perfection is almost non-existent and we confront complex scenarios [2].

The roots of MAS can be traced to early research in Distributed AI during the late 1970s and early 1980s. At that time, researchers began to challenge the assumption that intelligent behaviour must be centralised, instead proposing that collections of simpler problem-solving entities could collaboratively produce intelligent outcomes [3]. Early MAS were largely symbolic and rule-based, relying on explicitly defined knowledge representations and coordination mechanisms. These systems focused on distributed problem solving, cooperative task execution, and the decomposition of complex problems into smaller, manageable sub-problems that individual agents could address [4]. This period established many of the core theoretical concepts that continue to underpin MAS research today, including autonomy, coordination, and communication.

Throughout the 1990s, it evolved into a distinct and well-defined research field. During this period, agents were formally characterised by their ability to operate autonomously, respond to environmental changes, pursue long-term goals proactively, and engage in social interactions with other agents. Theoretical influences from game theory introduced rigorous frameworks for analysing strategic interaction, cooperation, and competition among agents, while insights from organisational theory informed models of coordination, hierarchy, and role assignment. At the same time, standardisation efforts led to the development of agent communication languages and interaction protocols, providing a common foundation for agent interoperability across heterogeneous systems [1].

As computational power increased and Machine Learning (ML) techniques matured, MAS research increasingly shifted toward adaptive and learning-based approaches. Reinforcement Learning enabled agents to learn optimal or near-optimal policies through interaction with the environment and other agents, while evolutionary methods allowed populations of agents to adapt collectively over time. Swarm intelligence, inspired by biological systems such as ant colonies and bird flocks, demonstrated how simple local rules could give rise to complex global behaviour without centralised control [5]. These developments highlighted the importance of emergence as a defining property of MAS, where system-level intelligence arises from interactions among agents rather than from any single agent's capabilities.

A defining aspect of MAS is inter-agent communication, which serves as the primary mechanism for agents to coordinate, negotiate, and adapt. Communication typically occurs through message passing, where agents exchange information about their beliefs, intentions, observations, or internal states. Messages may contain unstructured text, structured data representations, or complex objects such as learned models and executable plans [6]. Communication protocols specify not only the format of these messages but also their intended meaning and the expected responses, enabling agents to engage in structured interactions such as requests, commitments, negotiations, and agreements. Effective communication is essential for maintaining coherence and consistency in decentralised systems, particularly in environments characterised by uncertainty and partial observability [7].

Cooperation within MAS arises when agents share common goals or when achieving individual objectives depends on the successful coordination of multiple agents. Cooperative behaviour often involves the distribution of tasks, synchronisation of actions, and sharing of intermediate results or performance indicators. Agents may dynamically assume different roles based on their capabilities or the environment's current state, enabling the system to adapt to changing conditions. Theoretical models of cooperation emphasise mechanisms such as shared mental models and collective reward structures, all of which facilitate coordinated behaviour without centralised oversight. Cooperative MAS are widely used in domains such as robotics, sensor networks, and distributed decision support systems [8].

As MAS matured, a significant shift occurred with the integration of learning capabilities, fundamentally transforming how agents adapt, coordinate, and improve their behaviour over time. Early MAS relied on symbolic reasoning, predefined communication protocols, and hand-crafted coordination strategies, which limited their flexibility in dynamic or partially observable environments. The introduction of learning-based methods enabled agents to autonomously refine their policies through experience, allowing behaviour to emerge from interaction rather than explicit design [9].

The use of Deep Learning (DL) techniques integrated into the agents' pipelines enabled a more cohesive and intelligent approach to assessing each agent's individual tasks. This enables the creation of multiple agents that work cooperatively to apply DL models for classifying or predicting outcomes, which can then be used by other agents [10]. Several areas have explored such approaches, including financial markets and the coordination of patient care across multiple hospitals, to achieve maximum efficiency. This is only possible with access to large datasets for training several models that agents can use to infer, a process complicated by privacy laws and ethical considerations. Therefore, the next logical step is to apply another ML technique called RL [11].

RL provided a formal theoretical framework for this transition by modelling agent-environment interaction as a sequential decision-making process under uncertainty. In single-agent settings, RL demonstrated that optimal behaviour could be learned without prior knowledge of the environment's dynamics. Extending this framework to multi-agent contexts introduced fundamental theoretical challenges, most notably non-stationarity, since each agent's learning process alters the environment perceived by others. This challenge necessitated the development of Multi-Agent Reinforcement Learning (MARL), a research area concerned with the convergence, stability, and optimality of learning agents operating in shared environments [12].

From a theoretical perspective, Multi-Agent Reinforcement Learning (MARL) extends classical RL by incorporating concepts from game theory, dynamical systems, and control theory. Agents are no longer optimising against a static environment but are embedded in strategic settings where equilibria, best-response dynamics, and joint policy spaces become central analytical constructs. Cooperative MARL investigates how agents can learn joint policies that maximise shared objectives, while competitive MARL examines adversarial learning and strategic adaptation. Mixed-motive environments further complicate learning dynamics by requiring agents to balance collaboration with self-interest, reflecting many real-world scenarios [9].

The integration of DL into MARL significantly expanded agents' representational and functional capacities. Deep neural networks enabled agents to process high-dimensional sensory inputs, approximate complex value functions, and learn abstract representations of their environment and other agents. This advancement facilitated the emergence of sophisticated coordination strategies that could not be explicitly programmed. Importantly, it also enabled agents to learn not only how to act, but how to communicate [13].

Emergent communication represents a critical theoretical development in learning-based MAS. Rather than relying on predefined communication protocols or symbolic languages, agents learn communication strategies as part of their overall policy optimisation process [7]. Communication signals, initially arbitrary or uninterpretable, acquire meaning through their utility in improving coordination and collective performance. From an information-theoretic perspective, these signals function as learned encodings that reduce uncertainty about agents' internal states, intentions, or observations, thereby enabling more effective joint decision-making [14].

The study of these communication algorithms challenges traditional notions of language and semantics by demonstrating that meaningful communication can arise without explicit grounding in human language. Instead, semantics emerge implicitly through shared objectives and repeated interaction. Theoretical analyses of emergent communication draw upon concepts from signalling games, coordination games, and information bottleneck theory, framing communication as an adaptive mechanism shaped by environmental pressures and reward structures. These analyses reveal that communication protocols evolve to balance expressiveness, efficiency, and robustness, often exhibiting properties analogous to Natural Language Processing (NLP), such as compositionality and abstraction [15].

Emergent communication also has profound implications for the scalability and decentralisation of MAS. By enabling agents to exchange compressed, task-relevant information, communication reduces the need for centralised control or full observability. This allows MAS to operate effectively in large-scale environments with limited bandwidth and partial information, reinforcing the core MAS principle that global intelligence can arise from local interaction. Moreover, learned communication protocols can adapt as tasks and environments change, further enhancing system resilience and flexibility [16].

The progression from rule-based MAS to learning-enabled systems with emergent communication marks a decisive step toward more cognitively capable agent architectures. Agents are no longer confined to fixed interaction schemas but can develop shared representations, internal models of other agents, and adaptive coordination strategies. This theoretical evolution establishes a direct conceptual bridge to more advanced agent-based systems that emphasise reasoning, abstraction, and long-term planning, thereby setting the stage for the emergence of Agentic AI [17].

While emergent communication in learning-based MAS demonstrates that meaningful signalling can arise without explicit linguistic structure, it also reveals a natural limitation: the learned communication protocols are typically task-specific, opaque to humans, and difficult to transfer across domains [16]. These constraints highlight the need for communication mechanisms that are not only effective for coordination among agents but also interpretable, compositional, and generalisable. NLP, as a highly expressive and structured medium evolved for complex social coordination, provides a compelling solution to these challenges [18].

The integration of NLP into MAS fundamentally alters the nature of inter-agent communication. Unlike emergent symbolic signals, NLP enables agents to express abstract concepts, articulate intentions, reason about hypothetical scenarios, and communicate across tasks and domains. From a theoretical perspective, NLP can be viewed as a high-capacity communication channel that supports compositional semantics, allowing complex meanings to be constructed from simpler units. This compositionality enables agents to generalise knowledge and coordination strategies beyond narrowly defined environments, a property that is difficult to achieve with purely emergent communication protocols [19].

Recent advances in Large Language Models (LLMs) have made the use of NLP as a computational medium feasible within artificial agents. Trained on vast corpora of human-generated text, LLMs capture statistical regularities of language, encode world knowledge, and exhibit emergent reasoning capabilities. When embedded within agents, LLMs function not merely as language generators but as cognitive components capable of interpretation, planning, and decision support. This shift transforms language from a passive communication interface into an active substrate for reasoning and coordination [20].

From the perspective of MAS theory, LLM-enabled communication introduces a new class of agents whose internal representations and interaction protocols are grounded in NLP. Agents can exchange goals, constraints, plans, and explanations using shared linguistic abstractions, enabling a level of semantic alignment that was previously unattainable. This alignment reduces coordination complexity, as agents can reason about each other's intentions and strategies through explicit linguistic representations rather than inferring them indirectly from behaviour or learned signals [21].

The incorporation of LLMs also reshapes the theoretical boundaries between communication, cognition, and control. Traditional MAS architectures often treated communication as a separate layer, distinct from decision-making and action selection. In contrast, LLM-enabled agents integrate communication and reasoning within a unified representational framework, where language serves simultaneously as input, memory, and planning medium [22]. This integration enables agents to perform multi-step reasoning, decompose complex objectives into sub-goals, and adapt plans dynamically in response to new information from other agents or external systems.

These developments give rise to what is increasingly referred to as Agentic AI, a paradigm in which autonomous agents are centred around language-based reasoning capabilities. Agentic AI systems leverage LLMs to support goal formulation, long-term planning, self-reflection, and tool use, enabling agents to operate effectively in open-ended and human-centric environments. Within such systems, multiple agents may collaborate or compete by exchanging NLP messages that encode not only observations and actions but also beliefs, uncertainties, and justifications [23].

Theoretically, Agentic AI represents a convergence of MAS, NLP processing, and cognitive architectures. Core MAS principles such as autonomy, decentralisation, and emergence remain intact, but are extended through language-enabled reasoning and shared semantic spaces. NLP acts as a unifying abstraction layer that facilitates coordination among heterogeneous agents, including humans, software services, and embodied systems [24]. This convergence positions LLM-enabled Agentic AI as the most recent evolutionary stage of MAS, bridging decades of MAS theory with contemporary advances in ML and AI.

By grounding inter-agent communication and reasoning in NLP, Agentic AI systems transcend the limitations of task-specific emergent protocols, enabling scalable, interpretable, and adaptable intelligence. As a result, NLPâŁ"enabled agents are not merely communicative entities but participants in complex socio-technical systems, capable of collaboration, explanation, and alignment with human objectives. This shift marks a fundamental transformation in how intelligence is modelled and deployed within MAS, solidifying Agentic AI as a central concept in modern AI research [25].

The emergence of Agentic AI represents a significant evolution in the design and conceptualisation of MAS. Although classical MAS typically relied on predefined rules or narrowly scoped learning objectives, Agentic AI systems emphasise higher-level cognitive capabilities such as reasoning, planning, self-reflection, and goal decomposition [17]. These techniques can be attributed to advances in large language models, deep RL, and memory-augmented architectures, which have enabled agents to operate in open-ended environments, interact via NLP, and integrate information across time and modalities. In Agentic AI architectures, agents are often specialised according to function, such as perception, decision-making, execution, and explanation, forming coordinated networks of interacting intelligences [26].

From a theoretical standpoint, Agentic AI can be viewed as a convergence of MAS theory, cognitive architectures, and modern ML. Core MAS principles such as autonomy, decentralisation, communication, and emergence remain central, but are now augmented by probabilistic reasoning, neural representations, and self-adaptive control mechanisms [27]. This evolution raises new theoretical challenges related to scalability, alignment, trust, and interpretability, particularly as agentic systems increasingly interact with humans and operate in real-world settings. Nevertheless, the foundational concepts of MAS continue to provide a rigorous framework for understanding and designing Agentic AI, positioning MAS as a cornerstone in the theoretical foundations of modern intelligent systems [28].

## 2.2  Conceptual Integration

Agentic AI represents not merely a collection of advanced techniques but a conceptual integration of multiple strands of AI research into a unified paradigm. At its core, Agentic AI brings together autonomy, learning, reasoning, communication, and action within systems composed of interacting agents. Rather than treating these capabilities as independent modules, Agentic AI integrates them into cohesive agent-based architectures that operate continuously within dynamic environments, enabling intelligence to arise through sustained interaction rather than isolated computation [29].

This integration is most evident in how Agentic AI systems close the cognitive loop among perception, decision-making, action, and reflection. Agents perceive their environment and other agents' actions, reason about goals, constraints, and uncertainties, communicate using shared linguistic representations, and execute actions that modify both the environment and the collective system state [30]. Feedback from these actions is incorporated into subsequent reasoning and learning processes, allowing agents to adapt their behaviour over time. Crucially, this loop unfolds over extended temporal horizons, supported by persistent internal states and memory, which enable agents to accumulate experience, maintain identity continuity, and manage long-term objectives beyond immediate task execution [31].

A central element enabling this integration is NLP, which serves as a shared representational medium across agents and between agents and humans. Language provides a unifying abstraction layer through which goals, plans, beliefs, explanations, and uncertainties can be expressed, revised, and evaluated. Unlike low-level state representations or task-specific emergent communication protocols, NLP supports compositional reasoning and transfer across tasks and domains. As a result, agents coordinate through semantic alignment rather than explicit synchronisation, reducing coupling while increasing flexibility and interpretability [32].

From a system-level perspective, Agentic AI redefines intelligence as an emergent property of interaction rather than an isolated capability of individual components. Each agent may possess limited local knowledge, specialised skills, or partial observability, yet the collective system exhibits behaviours that exceed those of any single agent. Intelligence is thus distributed across the system, arising from communication, coordination, and mutual adaptation among agents [33]. This decentralised organisation enhances robustness and scalability, as agents can be added, removed, or reconfigured without undermining overall system coherence. Classical theoretical foundations from MAS remain central, but are extended through learning-based adaptation, language-mediated coordination, and long-term goal management [34].

Agentic AI also integrates planning, reasoning, and action into a unified adaptive process. Rather than separating these functions into distinct stages, agentic systems embed reasoning within action itself, continuously generating, evaluating, and revising plans as new information becomes available [35]. This tight coupling allows agents to respond effectively to uncertainty, incomplete knowledge, and changing objectives. Planning becomes an ongoing activity rather than a preliminary step, and reasoning serves not only to select actions but to interpret outcomes, detect failures, and adjust future behaviour [36].

A further dimension of conceptual integration lies in the role of humans within agentic systems. Agentic AI introduces a symmetry between human and artificial agents by grounding interaction in NLP, enabling both to participate within the same communicative and decision-making space [37]. Humans are no longer confined to external control or supervision; they can now act as collaborators, goal-setters, and sources of feedback within the agentic ecosystem. This integration supports human-in-the-loop operation while preserving agent autonomy, allowing guidance and oversight to emerge through dialogue rather than rigid control interfaces [38].

Explanation and self-reflection constitute additional integrative capabilities of Agentic AI. Agents are expected not only to act effectively but also to reason about their own behaviour, evaluate outcomes against goals, and articulate the rationale behind their decisions. This meta-cognitive capacity enhances transparency, trust, and collaboration, particularly in human-centric environments. Self-reflection enables agents to detect inconsistencies, revise assumptions, and adapt strategies, reinforcing long-term robustness and learning [39].

At a higher level of abstraction, Agentic AI can be understood as a shift from task-oriented intelligence to process-oriented intelligence. Rather than being optimised for single objectives or narrowly defined environments, agentic systems are designed to operate continuously, manage evolving goals, and remain coherent under changing conditions [40]. Success is measured not only by task completion but by adaptability, resilience, and sustained performance over time.

In this sense, Agentic AI synthesises decades of theoretical progress in AI into a coherent architectural vision. It integrates the decentralised coordination principles of MAS, the adaptability of learning-based agents, the expressive and unifying power of NLP, and the reflective capabilities of cognitive architectures. This conceptual integration establishes Agentic AI as a foundational framework for building intelligent systems capable of sustained autonomy, collective intelligence, meaningful human collaboration, and operation within complex real-world environments [17].

# References


1. Abdollah Amirkhani and Amir Hossein Barshooi. "Consensus in multi-agent systems: a review". In: *Artificial Intelligence Review* 55.5 (2022), pp. 3897–3935. DOI: https://doi.org/10.1007/s10462-021-10097-x.
2. Abdollah Amirkhani and Amir Hossein Barshooi. "Consensus in multi-agent systems: a review". In: *Artificial Intelligence Review* 55.5 (2022), pp. 3897–3935. DOI: https://doi.org/10.1007/s10462-021-10097-x.
3. J. Tweedale et al. "Innovations in multi-agent systems". In: *Journal of Network and Computer Applications* 30.3 (2007), pp. 1089–1115. ISSN: 1084-8045. DOI: https://doi.org/10.1016/j.jnca.2006.04.005.
4. Roberta Calegari et al. "Logic-based technologies for multi-agent systems: a systematic literature review". In: *Autonomous Agents and Multi-Agent Systems* 35.1 (2021), p. 1. DOI: https://doi.org/10.1007/s10458-020-09478-3.
5. Jun Tang, Haibin Duan, and Songyang Lao. "Swarm intelligence algorithms for multiple unmanned aerial vehicles collaboration: A comprehensive review". In: *Artificial Intelligence Review* 56.5 (2023), pp. 4295–4327. DOI: https://doi.org/10.1007/s10462-022-10281-7.
6. Jianrui Wang et al. "Integrated adaptive communication in multi-agent systems: Dynamic topology, frequency, and content optimization for efficient collaboration". In: *Neurocomputing* 617 (2025), p. 129068. ISSN: 0925-2312. DOI: https://doi.org/10.1016/j.neucom.2024.129068.
7. Abdollah Amirkhani and Amir Hossein Barshooi. "Consensus in multi-agent systems: a review". In: *Artificial Intelligence Review* 55.5 (2022), pp. 3897–3935. DOI: https://doi.org/10.1007/s10462-021-10097-x.

8. Jianrui Wang et al. "Cooperative and Competitive Multi-Agent Systems: From Optimization to Games". In: *IEEE/CAA Journal of Automatica Sinica* 9.5 (2022), pp. 763–783. DOI: https://doi.org/10.1109/JAS.2022.105506.

9. Lorenzo Canese et al. "Multi-agent reinforcement learning: A review of challenges and applications". In: *Applied Sciences* 11.11 (2021), p. 4948. DOI: https://doi.org/10.3390/app11114948.

10. Yutaka Matsuo et al. "Deep learning, reinforcement learning, and world models". In: *Neural Networks* 152 (2022), pp. 267–275. DOI: https://doi.org/10.1016/j.neunet.2022.03.037.

11. Ashish Kumar Shakya, Gopinatha Pillai, and Sohom Chakrabarty. "Reinforcement learning algorithms: A brief survey". In: *Expert Systems with Applications* 231 (2023), p. 120495. ISSN: 0957-4174. DOI: https://doi.org/10.1016/j.eswa.2023.120495.

12. Afshin Oroojlooy and Davood Hajinezhad. "A review of cooperative multi-agent deep reinforcement learning". In: *Applied Intelligence* 53.11 (2023), pp. 13677–13722. DOI: https://doi.org/10.1007/s10489-022-04105-y.

13. Wei Du and Shifei Ding. "A survey on multi-agent deep reinforcement learning: from the perspective of challenges and applications". In: *Artificial Intelligence Review* 54.5 (2021), pp. 3215–3238. DOI: https://doi.org/10.1007/s10462-020-09938-y.

14. Can Zhao et al. "Secure consensus of multi-agent systems with redundant signal and communication interference via distributed dynamic event-triggered control". In: *ISA Transactions* 112 (2021), pp. 89–98. ISSN: 0019-0578. DOI: https://doi.org/10.1016/j.isatra.2020.11.030.

15. Shivansh Patel et al. "Interpretation of Emergent Communication in Heterogeneous Collaborative Embodied Agents". In: *Proceedings of the IEEE/CVF International Conference on Computer Vision (ICCV)*. 2021, pp. 15953–15963.

16. Seth Karten et al. "Interpretable Learned Emergent Communication for Human–Agent Teams"". In: *IEEE Transactions on Cognitive and Developmental Systems* 15.4 (2023), pp. 1801–1811. DOI: https://doi.org/10.1109/TCDS.2023.3236599.

17. Ken Huang. *Agentic AI*. Springer, 2025. DOI: https://doi.org/10.1007/978-3-031-90026-6.

18. Diksha Khurana et al. "Natural language processing: state of the art, current trends and challenges". In: *Multimedia tools and applications* 82.3 (2023), pp. 3713–3744. DOI: https://doi.org/10.1007/s11042-022-13428-4.

19. Salvatore Claudio Fanni et al. "Natural Language Processing". In: *Introduction to Artificial Intelligence*. Ed. by Michail E. Klontzas, Salvatore Claudio Fanni, and Emanuele Neri. Cham: Springer International Publishing, 2023, pp. 87–99. ISBN: 978-3-031-25928-9. DOI: https://doi.org/10.1007/978-3-031-25928-9-5.

20. Yupeng Chang et al. "A survey on evaluation of large language models". In: *ACM transactions on intelligent systems and technology* 15.3 (2024), pp. 1–45. DOI: https://doi.org/10.1145/3641289.

21. Xinyi Li et al. "A survey on LLM-based multi-agent systems: workflow, infrastructure, and challenges". In: *Vicinagearth* 1.1 (2024), p. 9. DOI: https://doi.org/10.1007/s44336-024-00009-2.

22. Kostas Hatalis et al. "Memory matters: The need to improve long-term memory in llm-agents". In: *Proceedings of the AAAI Symposium Series*. Vol. 2. 1. 2023, pp. 277–280. DOI: https://doi.org/10.1609/aaaiss.v2i1.27688.

23. Xu Huang et al. *Understanding the planning of LLM agents: A survey*. 2024. DOI: https://doi.org/10.48550/arXiv.2402.02716. arXiv: 2402.02716 [cs.AI].

24. Adam Kostka and Jaros law A. Chudziak. *Towards Cognitive Synergy in LLM-Based Multi-Agent Systems: Integrating Theory of Mind and Critical Evaluation*. 2025. DOI: https://doi.org/10.48550/arXiv.2507.21969. arXiv: 2507.21969 [cs.MA].

25. Juan Mendoza-Collazos and Jordan Zlatev. "A cognitive-semiotic approach to agency: Assessing ideas from cognitive science and neuroscience". In: *Biosemiotics* 15.1 (2022), pp. 141–170. DOI: https://doi.org/10.1007/s12304-022-09473-z.

26. Tayiba Raheem and Gahangir Hossain. "Agentic AI Systems: Opportunities, Challenges, and Trustworthiness". In: *IEEE International Conference on Electro Information Technology (eIT)*. 2025, pp. 618–624. DOI: https://doi.org/10.1109/eIT64391.2025.11103638.

27. Thomas R. Caldwell. *The Agentic AI Bible*. Thomas R. Caldwell, 2025.
28. Anjanava Biswas and Wrick Talukdar. *Building Agentic AI Systems: Create intelligent, autonomous AI agents that can reason, plan, and adapt*. Packt Publishing Ltd, 2025. ISBN: 978-1803238753.
29. Ruichen Zhang et al. "Toward Edge General Intelligence With Agentic AI and Agentification: Concepts, Technologies, and Future Directions". In: *IEEE Communications Surveys & Tutorials* 28 (2026), pp. 4285–4318. DOI: https://doi.org/10.1109/COMST.2026.3651702.
30. Yogesh K. Dwivedi et al. "Agentic AI Systems: What It Is and Isn't". In: *Global Business and Organizational Excellence* n/a.n/a (). DOI: https://doi.org/10.1002/joe.70018.
31. Kamer Ali Yuksel et al. "A Multi—AI" Agent System for Autonomous Optimization of Agentic –AI" Solutions via Iterative Refinement and –LLM"-Driven Feedback Loops". In: *Proceedings of the 1st Workshop for Research on Agent Language Models (REALM 2025)*. Ed. by Ehsan Kamalloo et al. Vienna, Austria: Association for Computational Linguistics, July 2025, pp. 52–62. ISBN: 979-8-89176-264-0. DOI: https://doi.org/10.18653/v1/2025.realm-1.4.
32. Maxime Peyrard, Martin Josifoski, and Robert West. *Agentic AI: The Era of Semantic Decoding*. 2025. DOI: https://doi.org/10.48550/arXiv.2403.14562. arXiv: 2403.14562 [cs.CL].
33. Pengcheng Jiang et al. *Adaptation of Agentic AI*. 2025. DOI: https://doi.org/10.48550/arXiv.2512.16301. arXiv: 2512.16301 [cs.AI].
34. Laurie Hughes et al. "AI Agents and Agentic Systems: Redefining Global it Management". In: *Journal of Global Information Technology Management* 28.3 (2025), pp. 175–185. DOI: https://doi.org/10.1080/1097198X.2025.2524286.
35. Virginia Dignum and Frank Dignum. *Agentifying Agentic AI*. 2025. arXiv: 2511.17332 [cs.AI]. URL: https://arxiv.org/abs/2511.17332.
36. Ume Nisa et al. "Agentic AI: The age of reasoning–A review". In: *Journal of Automation and Intelligence* (2025). ISSN: 2949-8554. DOI: https://doi.org/10.1016/j.jai.2025.08.003.
37. Uwe M. Borghoff, Paolo Bottoni, and Remo Pareschi. "Human-artificial interaction in the age of agentic AI: a system-theoretical approach". In: *Frontiers in Human Dynamics* Volume 7 - 2025 (2025). ISSN: 2673-2726. DOI: https://doi.org/10.3389/fhumd.2025.1579166.
38. Paul M. Leonardi. "Homo agenticus in the age of agentic AI: Agency loops, power displacement, and the circulation of responsibility". In: *Information and Organization* 35.3 (2025), p. 100582. ISSN: 1471-7727. DOI: https://doi.org/10.1016/j.infoandorg.2025.100582.
39. Jeena Joseph. "The algorithmic self: how AI is reshaping human identity, introspection, and agency". In: *Frontiers in Psychology* Volume 16 - 2025 (2025). ISSN: 1664-1078. DOI: https://doi.org/10.3389/fpsyg.2025.1645795.
40. Hoang Vu et al. "Agentic business process management: practitioner perspectives on agent governance in business processes". In: *International Conference on Business Process Management*. Springer. 2025, pp. 29–43. DOI: https://doi.org/10.1007/978-3-032-02936-2-3.

# Chapter 3
# Architectural Design Principles

**Abstract** This chapter translates the theoretical foundations of Agentic Artificial Intelligence (AI) into concrete architectural design principles. It presents a modular view of agentic systems, outlining the functional roles of perception, reasoning, learning, communication, and control within individual agents and across agent collectives. The chapter explores orchestration strategies that enable coordination among heterogeneous agents while maintaining decentralised autonomy. Design considerations such as scalability, robustness, and adaptability are examined, with particular attention to how language-based reasoning and learning components are embedded within agent architectures. It provides a systematic framework for designing agentic systems that support long-term operation, collaborative problem-solving, and dynamic reconfiguration, along with detailed descriptions of the different frameworks.

## 3.1 Principles of Agentic System Design

Designing an agentic system requires rethinking conventional architectural assumptions in AI and software engineering. Instead of modelling intelligence as a static function or a centrally controlled pipeline, agentic system design treats intelligence as an ongoing process that emerges from the interaction, adaptation, and coordination among autonomous agents. The architectural focus therefore shifts from optimising isolated components to orchestrating behaviour over time, under uncertainty, and across multiple interacting entities [1].

A foundational principle of agentic system design is autonomy through encapsulation. Agents are constructed as self-contained units with their own goals, reasoning processes, and decision-making logic. This encapsulation allows agents to operate independently while remaining responsive to shared objectives and environmental feedback. Autonomy is not synonymous with isolation; rather, it presupposes structured interaction. Effective agentic architectures, therefore, define clear boundaries between agents while simultaneously providing rich communication channels through which coordination can occur [2].



P. Oliveira et al., *Architectures for Agentic AI*, SpringerBriefs in Intelligent Systems,
https://doi.org/10.1007/978-3-032-24781-0_3

Another core principle is functional specialisation. Agentic systems are most effective when complex objectives are decomposed into distinct cognitive and operational roles. This decomposition enables scalability, interpretability, and fault tolerance, as individual agents can be improved or replaced without destabilising the system as a whole [3]. Importantly, specialisation does not imply rigid task assignment. In advanced agentic systems, roles may be dynamic, with agents adapting their responsibilities based on system state and performance feedback [4]. These abstract principles are thereby instantiated in different ways by contemporary agentic frameworks. LangChain, AutoGen, and CrewAI exemplify distinct design philosophies, each prioritising different aspects of autonomy, coordination, and control. Understanding these frameworks in depth provides valuable insight into the broader design space of agentic systems [5].

LangChain represents an architectural approach rooted in compositionality and controlled execution. Its core abstraction is the chain, which structures reasoning as a sequence or graph of modular components such as prompts, memory units, retrievers, and tools. From an agentic perspective, LangChain offers a high degree of transparency and control, as each step in the reasoning process is explicitly defined and can be inspected. This makes it particularly well-suited for applications where reproducibility, traceability, and deterministic behaviour are essential [6].

It also supports agent-like behaviour through constructs that allow dynamic tool selection and conditional execution, enabling limited autonomy within a bounded execution space. However, this autonomy remains tightly coupled to a predefined orchestration structure. Agents in LangChain do not typically negotiate, critique one another, or adapt their roles through interaction. As a result, LangChain aligns more closely with single-agent or centrally coordinated multi-component systems than with fully decentralised multi-agent architectures. Its strengths lie in integrating external knowledge sources, enforcing reasoning constraints, and supporting structured workflows, while its limitations emerge in scenarios requiring emergent cooperation, long-term autonomy, or open-ended interaction among multiple agents [7].

In opposition to AutoGen, which adopts a markedly different design philosophy, placing conversational interaction at the centre of agentic behaviour. In AutoGen, agents are defined primarily by their communicative capabilities and behavioural policies, with interaction unfolding through Natural Language Processing (NLP) dialogue. This design closely mirrors theoretical models of decentralised intelligence, in which coordination and problem-solving emerge from iterative exchange rather than from predefined control flow. Agents in AutoGen can reason, critique, propose alternatives, and revise their behaviour in response to feedback from other agents [8].

A defining feature of AutoGen is its support for reflection and self-correction through dialogue. Agents can evaluate one another's outputs, challenge assumptions, and converge toward improved solutions over time. This makes AutoGen particularly suitable for complex reasoning tasks, exploratory problem solving, and systems where explanation quality and interpretability are critical. However, the very flexibility that enables emergence also introduces challenges [9]. System behaviour can become difficult to predict, and without carefully designed termination conditions, evaluation criteria, and role definitions, agent interactions may drift or loop indefinitely. AutoGen, therefore, demands careful architectural discipline to balance openness with control [8].

CrewAI occupies an intermediate position between orchestration-driven and fully emergent agentic systems. Its design is inspired by human team structures, explicitly modelling agents as crew members with defined roles, responsibilities, and goals. Task allocation and coordination are guided by these role definitions, enabling efficient collaboration without requiring constant negotiation. From a design perspective, CrewAI excels in scenarios where tasks can be clearly decomposed and where cooperative behaviour follows predictable patterns [10].

The strength of CrewAI lies in its clarity and accessibility. Explicitly encoding roles and objectives simplifies system design and reduces the cognitive overhead of managing complex agent interactions. This makes it well-suited for applied settings such as document generation, decision support, and structured analytical workflows [11]. However, the reliance on predefined roles can constrain adaptability. In highly dynamic environments or tasks requiring creative or adversarial interaction, CrewAI's structured collaboration model may limit the emergence of novel strategies or behaviours [10].

Comparing these frameworks reveals a fundamental tension in agentic system design between control and emergence. LangChain prioritises structure and predictability, making it ideal for systems where reliability and auditability are paramount. AutoGen prioritises interaction and adaptability, enabling rich emergent behaviour at the cost of increased complexity. CrewAI offers a pragmatic compromise, supporting cooperative multi-agent behaviour through explicit role definition while retaining some flexibility [12].

The choice among these frameworks, or the decision to combine elements from multiple approaches, should be guided by the intended operational context of the agentic system. Systems operating in regulated or safety-critical domains may benefit from tighter orchestration, while systems aimed at exploration, explanation, or collaboration may require greater decentralisation and communicative richness. Crucially, these frameworks should not be viewed as mutually exclusive solutions, but as reference architectures that illuminate different points in the agentic design space [13].

Overall, the principles of agentic system design are realised through architectural decisions that govern autonomy, coordination, communication, and learning. LangChain, AutoGen, and CrewAI exemplify distinct interpretations of these principles, each offering valuable insights into how agentic intelligence can be structured and operationalised. A deep understanding of these frameworks enables designers to construct agentic systems that are not only technically effective but conceptually aligned with the goals of sustained autonomy, adaptability, and meaningful interaction.

## 3.2  Agent Typologies

Agent typologies provide a crucial conceptual layer in the design of agentic systems, as they determine how responsibilities, reasoning processes, and interactions are distributed across the system. In Agentic AI, agents are not merely execution units but encapsulate distinct cognitive roles, each optimised for particular forms of decision-making, interaction, and adaptation. Modern agentic frameworks such as LangChain, CrewAI, and AutoGen formalise these roles through predefined agent types, offering designers a structured vocabulary for mapping abstract principles into concrete system components [12].

Within LangChain, agent typologies are primarily centred around reasoning strategies and tool interaction patterns. The Zero-shot ReAct agent exemplifies a tightly integrated reasoning-and-action loop, in which the agent alternates between internal reasoning steps and external tool use without prior task-specific examples. This agent type is particularly useful in open-ended problem-solving scenarios where the sequence of actions cannot be predefined, such as exploratory analysis, dynamic information retrieval, or question answering over heterogeneous data sources. Its strength lies in flexibility, though this comes at the cost of reduced predictability and control in long-running workflows [14].

The Conversational Agent in LangChain extends this paradigm by incorporating dialogue history as a first-class component of reasoning. This agent is well-suited for interactive systems where continuity, context retention, and user engagement are essential, such as conversational assistants or decision-support interfaces. Grounding reasoning in conversational state enables more coherent multi-turn interactions but may be less effective for tasks requiring deep planning beyond the conversational horizon [15].

The Self-ask with Search agent introduces explicit decomposition into sub-questions, allowing the agent to query external knowledge sources iteratively. This agent type is especially effective for factual reasoning tasks that depend on reliable external information, such as knowledge-intensive question answering or validation of uncertain claims [16]. Its structured decomposition improves transparency and correctness, though it may be less efficient for tasks requiring creative synthesis rather than factual grounding.

LangChain's Modular Reasoning, Knowledge & Language (MRKL) agent, which combines modular reasoning, knowledge access, and learning, is designed for environments where multiple specialised tools or knowledge bases must be orchestrated. This agent is useful in complex systems that require routing sub-tasks to domain-specific modules, such as hybrid symbolicâ€"neural pipelines or enterprise knowledge systems. Finally, the Tool-using Agent generalises this idea by explicitly focusing on selecting and invoking tools during the reasoning process, making it particularly suitable for automation workflows, Application Programming Interface (API)-driven systems, and task-execution environments [6].

CrewAI approaches agent typologies from an organisational and behavioural perspective, emphasising role specialisation and collaboration. Reactive agents in CrewAI prioritise immediate response to environmental stimuli or task triggers, making them well-suited for monitoring, validation, and lightweight decision-making where speed and simplicity are paramount. These agents sacrifice long-term planning in favour of responsiveness, aligning closely with reflexive behaviour observed in biological and organisational systems [17].

Planning agents in CrewAI explicitly model goal decomposition and sequencing, enabling them to construct multi-step plans before execution. This makes them particularly effective for complex workflows with dependencies, such as data pipelines, multi-stage analysis, or coordinated task execution across agents. Learning agents extend this capability by adapting their behaviour over time based on feedback, allowing systems to improve performance across repeated executions. These agents are especially valuable in non-stationary environments where static strategies quickly become suboptimal [18].

Collaborative agents in CrewAI operate as part of a team, sharing information, negotiating responsibilities, and coordinating actions. They are most useful in systems where no single agent has sufficient information or capability to complete the task independently, reflecting real-world organisational structures. Goal-oriented agents focus on maintaining alignment with high-level objectives, making them suitable for systems that must operate over long horizons while adapting to changing constraints. Reflexive agents, finally, incorporate self-evaluation mechanisms, enabling them to critique and adjust their own outputs, which is particularly useful for quality assurance, iterative refinement, and safety-critical applications [10].

AutoGen defines agent typologies primarily through communication roles and interaction patterns, reflecting its emphasis on dialogue-driven coordination. The ConversableAgent represents a general-purpose communicative entity capable of engaging in structured or unstructured dialogue. This agent type is useful as a flexible building block in systems where communication itself drives coordination, such as negotiation, explanation generation, or collaborative reasoning [8].

The AssistantAgent is specialised for task execution and problem-solving, typically operating under instructions received through dialogue. It is particularly effective for analytical tasks, content generation, and decision support, where the agent must interpret natural-language goals and produce actionable outputs. The UserProxyAgent explicitly models human participation within the agentic system, acting as an interface for user intent, approval, or intervention. This agent type is especially valuable in human-in-the-loop systems, ensuring that human oversight and guidance are structurally embedded rather than treated as external assumptions [19].

Finally, the GroupChatManager coordinates interactions among multiple agents, managing turn-taking, message routing, and conversational structure. This agent is crucial in multi-agent settings where coherence and coordination must be maintained across parallel interactions, such as collaborative problem-solving or multi-perspective evaluation. Its role highlights a key insight of Agentic AI: that orchestration and communication are themselves first-class cognitive functions [20].

Across these frameworks, agent typologies serve not merely as implementation conveniences but as design abstractions that encode assumptions about cognition, coordination, and control. Choosing an appropriate agent type is therefore a conceptual decision as much as a technical one, requiring alignment between the agent's capabilities and the role it is expected to fulfil within the broader system. By making these roles explicit, agentic frameworks enable designers to systematically translate high-level principles, such as autonomy, cooperation, and reflection, into concrete architectural components.

## 3.3  Communication and Cooperation Mechanisms

Communication and cooperation constitute the operational backbone of agentic systems. While autonomy allows individual agents to act independently, meaningful intelligence at the system level emerges only when agents can exchange information, coordinate decisions, and adapt collectively [21]. In Agentic AI, communication is not merely a data-transfer mechanism but a cognitive process through which agents align goals, negotiate responsibilities, and construct shared understanding. Contemporary agentic frameworks differ significantly in how they formalise and support these interactions, reflecting distinct design philosophies about cooperation and control [13].

LangChain adopts a minimalistic approach to communication, relying primarily on direct message passing between agents. Messages typically contain NLP instructions, intermediate reasoning steps, or structured outputs that are passed sequentially between agents. This simplicity aligns with LangChain's emphasis on composability and transparency: agents communicate just enough information to enable the next reasoning or execution step without imposing rigid interaction protocols. Such an approach is particularly effective in linear or semi-linear workflows, where the flow of control is largely predetermined, and agents operate in a loosely coupled manner [22]. However, because LangChain does not natively encode explicit cooperation strategies, collaborative behaviour must be designed externally by the system architect. Cooperation, therefore, emerges implicitly through prompt design and message sequencing rather than through built-in negotiation or delegation mechanisms [7].

In contrast, CrewAI treats cooperation as a first-class design concern. Its communication model is explicitly oriented toward collaborative task execution, mirroring human organisational structures. Agents in CrewAI interact through collaboration tools that allow them to delegate work or request information from one another. The Delegate Work Tool enables an agent to assign a sub-task to another agent based on their role or expertise, effectively distributing responsibility across the system. This mechanism is particularly useful in complex tasks that require decomposition, parallel execution, or specialisation, as it allows agents to offload work rather than attempting to solve everything independently [23].

In addition to delegation, the Ask Question Tool allows agents to query one another for clarification, context, or intermediate results. This form of interaction supports cooperative reasoning by enabling agents to reduce uncertainty and align their actions without central coordination. Together, these tools enable CrewAI systems to exhibit structured collaboration, where cooperation is not an emergent side effect but an explicit operational capability. This makes CrewAI especially suitable for long-running workflows, multi-step problem-solving, and scenarios where coordination overhead must be managed systematically [18].

When observing another framework, such as AutoGen, that adopts a communication-centric view of agentic cooperation, positioning dialogue itself as the primary mechanism through which coordination and intelligence emerge. Agents communicate by sending messages either directly to one another or within a GroupChat, a shared conversational space managed by a dedicated coordination agent. This design allows multiple agents to participate in a common dialogue, observe each other's contributions, and adjust their behaviour accordingly. Such shared conversational contexts are particularly effective for collaborative reasoning, debate, evaluation, and iterative refinement, where visibility into others' reasoning processes enhances collective performance [12].

A distinctive feature of AutoGen is its event-driven communication model. Agents can be programmed with 'on_message' handlers that trigger specific actions when particular messages are received [20]. When no explicit handler is defined, the agent defaults to using its underlying Large Language Models (LLM) to interpret the message and generate an appropriate response. This hybrid approach enables a seamless integration of deterministic behaviour and generative reasoning, allowing designers to precisely control certain interactions while leaving others open-ended. As a result, AutoGen systems can support both tightly controlled workflows and emergent cooperative dynamics within the same architecture [13].

From a conceptual perspective, these communication mechanisms reflect different interpretations of cooperation in Agentic AI. LangChain prioritises simplicity and composability, enabling lightweight coordination through message passing but leaving cooperation largely implicit. CrewAI embeds cooperation directly into the agent model, providing explicit tools for delegation and inquiry that support structured collaboration. AutoGen elevates communication to a central organising principle, using dialogue as both a coordination mechanism and a medium for collective reasoning [12].

Across all three frameworks, communication serves as the foundation for cooperation. Whether minimalistic, tool-driven, or dialogue-centric, these mechanisms determine how agents share knowledge, distribute responsibilities, and converge toward shared objectives. Understanding these differences is essential for designing agentic systems that balance autonomy with coordination, and for selecting the appropriate framework based on the complexity, openness, and collaborative demands of the target application.

## 3.4  Orchestration and Control Layers

Orchestration and control layers define how autonomy is structured within an agentic system. While individual agents may act independently, effective agentic architectures require mechanisms that guide task allocation, regulate interaction, and ensure coherence toward system-level objectives. In Agentic AI, orchestration does not imply rigid centralisation but rather the intentional design of control structures that balance flexibility with accountability. The frameworks considered in this work implement orchestration through distinct architectural paradigms, each reflecting a different stance on how agents should be governed [24].

In the LangChain ecosystem, it employs a hierarchical orchestration model centred around a Lead Agent. This agent functions as the primary coordinator, receiving the user's high-level query and decomposing it into a sequence of well-defined subtasks. Rather than executing these subtasks itself, the Lead Agent assigns them to specialised subagents, effectively acting as a cognitive planner and dispatcher. The success of this orchestration strategy depends heavily on how each subagent is specified. Each subagent must be given a clear objective, an explicit description of the expected output format, guidance on which tools or information sources it may use, and strict task boundaries that prevent scope creep or unintended overlap with other agents.

This design enforces a disciplined form of autonomy, where agents operate independently but within carefully defined constraints. Control is achieved not through runtime intervention but through precise task specification at design time [15]. As a result, LangChain's orchestration layer is highly predictable and transparent, making it well-suited for deterministic workflows and applications where traceability and reproducibility are critical. However, because the Lead Agent retains responsibility for task decomposition, adaptability to unexpected situations or dynamic re-planning must be explicitly engineered, limiting emergent coordination [18].

However, CrewAI approaches orchestration through role-based control rather than explicit hierarchical command. Each agent is assigned a clearly defined role and a specific objective, which together determine its scope of responsibility within the system. Once roles are established, agents operate with a high degree of independence, focusing exclusively on their assigned tasks without needing continuous oversight. Orchestration in CrewAI is therefore implicit in the system's role structure: control emerges from the alignment of agent roles with the overall mission rather than from a central planning entity [10].

The aforementioned role-driven orchestration closely mirrors organisational and socio-technical models, where individuals are trusted to execute their responsibilities autonomously while contributing to a collective goal. It is particularly effective in complex, multi-stage workflows where task ownership must be stable over time. By constraining agents through role definitions and objectives, CrewAI reduces coordination overhead and minimises conflicts between agents. At the same time, this approach enables flexible collaboration, as agents can still delegate tasks or seek information when necessary without violating the overall control structure [23].

As opposed to AutoGen, which adopts a conversational orchestration model that combines decentralised autonomy with managed interaction. Control is exercised through a GroupChat environment overseen by a GroupChatManager. Each agent in the system is assigned a specific role and task, but rather than operating in isolation, they publish their outputs, reasoning, and responses into a shared conversational space. The GroupChatManager serves as an orchestration layer that governs participation, determining which agent may speak at a given moment and ensuring the dialogue progresses toward the intended objective.

Here, the design shifts control from task assignment to interaction regulation. Rather than prescribing a fixed execution order, AutoGen enables agents to reason collectively through structured dialogue, with the GroupChatManager maintaining coherence and preventing unproductive or redundant exchanges [19]. Such an orchestration model is particularly well-suited for open-ended tasks, evaluation loops, and reflective reasoning, where the order and content of agent contributions cannot be fully specified in advance. Control is therefore adaptive, responding dynamically to the evolving conversational context.

Across these frameworks, orchestration and control are implemented not as monolithic command structures but as architectural patterns that shape agent behaviour. LangChain emphasises hierarchical planning and strict task specification; CrewAI relies on role-based governance and objective alignment; and AutoGen orchestrates interactions through managed dialogue. Together, these approaches illustrate the design space of agentic control layers, demonstrating how different orchestration strategies can support varying degrees of autonomy, adaptability, and emergent intelligence. In practical agentic systems, the choice of orchestration model fundamentally influences scalability, robustness, and the system's capacity to operate effectively in complex and uncertain environments.

# References


1. Jeyoon Lee et al. "Agentic Built Environments: a review". In: *Energy and Buildings* 346 (2025), p. 116159. ISSN: 0378-7788. DOI: https://doi.org/10.1016/j.enbuild.2025.116159.
2. Laurie Hughes et al. "AI Agents and Agentic Systems: A Multi-Expert Analysis". In: *Journal of Computer Information Systems* 65.4 (2025), pp. 489–517. DOI: https://doi.org/10.1080/08874417.2025.2483832.
3. Jinyuan Fang et al. *A Comprehensive Survey of Self-Evolving AI Agents: A New Paradigm Bridging Foundation Models and Lifelong Agentic Systems*. 2025. DOI: https://doi.org/10.48550/arXiv.2508.07407. arXiv: 2508.07407 [cs.AI].
4. Soodeh Hosseini and Hossein Seilani. "The role of agentic AI in shaping a smart future: A systematic review". In: *Array* 26 (2025), p. 100399. ISSN: 2590-0056. DOI: https://doi.org/10.1016/j.array.2025.100399.
5. Hana Derouiche, Zaki Brahmi, and Haithem Mazeni. *Agentic AI Frameworks: Architectures, Protocols, and Design Challenges*. 2025. DOI: https://doi.org/10.48550/arXiv.2508.10146. arXiv: 2508.10146 [cs.AI].
6. Sangeetha Annam et al. "LangChain". In: *Textual Intelligence*. John Wiley & Sons, Ltd, 2025. Chap. 12, pp. 287–304. ISBN: 9781394287499. DOI: https://doi.org/10.1002/9781394287499.ch12.
7. Rakha Asyrofi et al. "Systematic Literature Review Langchain Proposed". In: *International Electronics Symposium (IES)*. 2023, pp. 533–537. DOI: https://doi.org/10.1109/IES59143.2023.10242497.
8. Rafael Barbarroxa et al. "Benchmarking AutoGen with different large language models". In: *IEEE Conference on Artificial Intelligence (CAI)*. 2024, pp. 263–264. DOI: https://doi.org/10.1109/CAI59869.2024.00058.

9.  Qingyun Wu et al. *AutoGen: Enabling Next-Gen LLM Applications via Multi-Agent Conversation*. 2023. DOI: https://doi.org/10.48550/arXiv.2308.08155. arXiv: 2308.08155 [cs.AI].

10. P Venkadesh, SV Divya, and K Subash Kumar. "Unlocking ai creativity: A multi-agent approach with crewai". In: *Journal of Trends in Computer Science Smart Technology* 6.4 (2024), pp. 338–356. DOI: https://doi.org/10.36548/jtcsst.2024.4.002.

11. Tom Taulli and Gaurav Deshmukh. "CrewAI". In: *Building Generative AI Agents: Using Lang-Graph, AutoGen, and CrewAI*. Springer, 2025, pp. 103–145. DOI: https://doi.org/10.1007/979-8-8688-1134-0_6.

12. Shuang Ying Chin and Dr Ng Kok Why. "Comparative of Multi-Agent System Frameworks: Crewai, Langchain, and Autogen". In: *Langchain, and Autogen* (2024). DOI: https://doi.org/10.2139/ssrn.5367964.

13. Seok-Hyang Cho and Yo-Seob Lee. "A Comparative Study of Modern AI Frameworks Based on Architecture, Integration, and Scalability". In: *International journal of advanced smart convergence* 14.4 (2025), pp. 158–167. DOI: https://doi.org/10.7236/IJASC.2025.14.4.158.

14. Dharin Dave et al. "Learning in LangChain". In: *World Congress on Smart Computing: Proceedings of WCSC 2024*. Springer Nature. 2025, p. 29. DOI: https://doi.org/10.1007/978-981-97-9006-7_3.

15. Deepti Goyal and Amita Gautam. "Introduction to LangChain Framework". In: *Textual Intelligence*. John Wiley & Sons, Ltd, 2025. Chap. 11, pp. 253–285. ISBN: 9781394287499. DOI: https://doi.org/10.1002/9781394287499.ch11.

16. Rabi Jay. "Introduction to LangChain and LLMs". In: *Generative AI Apps with LangChain and Python: A Project-Based Approach to Building Real-World LLM Apps*. Springer, 2024, pp. 1–38. DOI: https://doi.org/10.1007/979-8-8688-0882-1_1.

17. Vinay Pratap Karwal et al. "Multi-agent AI Framework for Developer Assistance: A New Paradigm in Software Engineering Automation". In: *International Conference on Data Analytics & Management*. Springer. 2025, pp. 229–242. DOI: https://doi.org/10.1007/978-3-032-03769-5_18.

18. Daniel Liu et al. "A Large-Scale Study on the Development and Issues of Multi-Agent AI Systems". In: *arXiv preprint* arXiv:2601.07136 (2026). DOI: https://doi.org/10.48550/arXiv.2601.07136.

19. Tom Taulli and Gaurav Deshmukh. "AutoGen". In: *Building Generative AI Agents: Using LangGraph, AutoGen, and CrewAI*. Springer, 2025, pp. 147–177. DOI: https://doi.org/10.1007/979-8-8688-1134-0_7.

20. Guangyao Chen et al. "Autoagents: A framework for automatic agent generation". In: *arXiv preprint* arXiv:2309.17288 (2023). DOI: https://doi.org/10.48550/arXiv.2309.17288.

21. Feibo Jiang et al. "From large ai models to agentic ai: A tutorial on future intelligent communications". In: *arXiv preprint* arXiv:2505.22311 (2025). DOI: https://doi.org/10.48550/arXiv.2505.22311.

22. Gaurav Samdani, Yawal Dixit, and Ganesh Viswanathan. "Leveraging LangGraph and Auto-Gen for Agentic AI Frameworks". In: *World Journal of Advanced Engineering Technology and Sciences* (2023). DOI: https://doi.org/10.30574/wjaets.2023.8.2.0068.

23. Rafael Barbarroxa, Luis Gomes, and Zita Vale. "Benchmarking large language models for multi-agent systems: A comparative analysis of autogen, crewai, and taskweaver". In: *International Conference on Practical Applications of Agents and Multi-Agent Systems*. Springer. 2024, pp. 39–48. DOI: https://doi.org/10.1007/978-3-031-70415-4_4.

24. Charlie Masters et al. "Orchestrating Human-AI Teams: The Manager Agent as aUnifying Research Challenge". In: *Proceedings of the 2025 7th International Conference on Distributed Artificial Intelligence*. DAI '25. New York, NY, USA: Association for Computing Machinery, 2025, pp. 91–107. ISBN: 9798400722752. DOI: https://doi.org/10.1145/3772429.3772439.

# Chapter 4
# Language-Based Interpretability in Agentic Systems

**Abstract** This chapter addresses the challenge of interpretability in Agentic Artificial Intelligence (AI), focusing on how autonomous, learning-enabled systems can remain transparent and accountable. It examines the limitations of traditional post-hoc explainability techniques in complex, multi-agent environments. The chapter introduces language-based interpretability as an intrinsic mechanism through which agents can articulate reasoning processes, decisions, and uncertainties. By embedding explanation capabilities within agent architectures, agentic systems enable continuous human-AI interaction and collaborative oversight. The discussion highlights how interpretability supports trust, error diagnosis, and system governance, particularly in safety-critical and environmental applications. The chapter positions interpretability not as an auxiliary feature, but as a core design requirement for sustainable and responsible Agentic AI.

## 4.1 Foundations of Interpretability in AI

Interpretability has become a central theme in modern AI research. As AI systems increasingly influence high-risk domains, such as healthcare diagnostics, environmental monitoring, autonomous systems, finance, and public decision-making, the need to understand how these systems arrive at their conclusions has grown [1]. Interpretability provides the means to bridge the gap between the complexity of AI models and the human users who must trust, evaluate, and often act upon their results. At its core, interpretability refers to the extent to which a human can understand how the system arrived at the final result and explain its reasoning process. Although simpler models, such as linear regression or decision trees, have traditionally been considered inherently interpretable, the rapid shift toward complex, multi-layered architectures, particularly Deep Learning (DL) and ensemble methods, has made interpretability a scientific challenge in its own right [2].

Historically, the demand for interpretability was relatively modest because early Machine Learning (ML) systems operated primarily in research contexts or in low-risk applications. These were also constructed following rule-based approaches, making them interpretable at their core. However, as ML has become much more complex, for example by combining different architectures and creating hybrid systems, its interpretation has become even more complicated [3]. In addition, these were embedded in operational pipelines, real-time decision systems, and policy-relevant scenarios, making their opacity increasingly problematic. This shift sparked the broader movement known as Explainable Artificial Intelligence (XAI). The goal of XAI is to develop methods, algorithms, and conceptual frameworks that make the behaviour of AI models transparent and understandable without sacrificing predictive performance. XAI is still a relatively young and actively evolving field, marked by diverging definitions, incomplete theoretical foundations, and ongoing debates around what it means for a model to be "truly interpretable." Nevertheless, it has produced a wide variety of methodologies to demystify complex systems [4].

One of the earliest foundations of interpretability concerns the distinction between intrinsic and post-hoc interpretability. Intrinsic interpretability refers to models whose structure is naturally understandable. Linear models, logistic regression and shallow decision trees fall into this category. Their interpretability arises from the fact that the relationship between inputs and outputs can be directly inspected [5]. For example, coefficients describe the contribution of each feature, and decision rules describe the path from the inputs to the prediction. However, these models often struggle to capture the high-dimensional, nonlinear relationships that deep neural networks or ensembles can model. As a result, intrinsic interpretability is frequently traded for increasing performance [6].

This led to the rise of post-hoc interpretability, in which explanations are generated after the model has produced a final result [7]. These explanations focus not on the model's full internal workings, but on providing insights that approximate or summarise its behaviour. Popular methods include saliency maps, partial dependence plots, counterfactual examples, feature attribution methods such as SHapley Additive exPlanations (SHAP) and Local Interpretable Model-agnostic Explanations (LIME), concept-based explanations, and surrogate models. Each of these approaches serves different interpretability goals: some aim to identify influential features, others to show the effect of modifying specific variables, while others aim to highlight the internal representations the model has learned [8].

Despite these advances, interpretability remains a fundamentally difficult scientific problem. One challenge is the mismatch between machine and human reasoning [9]. Deep neural networks represent information in high-dimensional spaces that humans cannot intuitively grasp. Another challenge lies in the ambiguity of the term "explanation" [10]. An explanation can mean a mathematical justification, a causal account, a simplification, or even a narrative tailored to a user's cognitive needs. These differences make it difficult to evaluate explanations or measure their fidelity to the underlying model.

Additionally, the field is grappling with the tension between interpretability and performance. Even though high-capacity models can uncover complex patterns, explaining their behaviour often requires simplifying assumptions that may not fully reflect their true reasoning. There is also growing awareness of "deceptive interpretability", in which an explanation appears plausible but does not accurately reflect the system's internal mechanisms [11]. This risk has prompted researchers to develop more rigorous interpretability tools grounded in statistical, causal, and information-theoretic principles.

Lately, interpretability research has shifted away from model-centric approaches toward more holistic perspectives. Instead of asking solely how a model makes decisions, researchers also ask how it should communicate those decisions in ways that align with human understanding, domain expectations, and organisational contexts [12]. This includes integrating interpretability directly into decision-support pipelines, regulatory frameworks, and human-AI collaboration systems. In fields such as environmental science or healthcare, where complex numerical models produce long chains of transformations, the need for interpretable outputs becomes even more essential [13].

XAI is also entering a new stage, with classical methods increasingly being supplemented or even reimagined by Large Language Models (LLMs). Although this transition is discussed in later sections, it is important to recognise here that the emergence of LLMs has significantly expanded the scope of interpretability research [14]. Instead of relying solely on pre-defined mathematical techniques, interpretability can now be enhanced through Natural Language Processing (NLP) explanations, interactive reasoning, and contextual interpretation of complex model behaviours [15]. This illustrates the broader trajectory of the field, from purely algorithmic explanations to communicative, adaptive, and aligned with human reasoning processes.

At the same time, interpretability research is being reshaped by new constraints and opportunities in modern AI ecosystems. The development of real-time applications demands explanations that are both accurate and efficient. The rise of small, domain-specific language models and resource-constrained deployments also redefines which interpretability mechanisms are feasible. These changes indicate that interpretability is no longer an isolated research topic but a core component of robust AI system design [16]. In this sense, foundational interpretability sets the stage for the more advanced mechanisms explored later in this chapter, including the integration of LLMs into Agentic AI frameworks that operationalise interpretability within the decision-making pipeline.

## 4.2  Large Language Models for Interpretability

LLM introduce a fundamentally different paradigm for interpretability by shifting the focus from purely mathematical explanations to linguistic and contextual reasoning [17]. Unlike traditional XAI methods that rely on predefined visualisations, feature attributions, or surrogate models, LLMs operate as interpretive interfaces that translate complex model behaviour into human-understandable narratives [18]. This capability enables AI systems to explain not only what decision was made, but also why it may have been made, in a form that aligns with human cognitive and communicative processes.

One of the primary contributions of LLMs to interpretability is their ability to serve as semantic translators. Modern AI pipelines often involve multiple components, such as data preprocessing, feature engineering, deep learning models, post-processing rules, and decision thresholds [19]. While each component may be technically interpretable in isolation, the overall system behaviour is difficult for end-users to comprehend. LLMs can integrate structured outputs from these components and generate coherent explanations that summarise the end-to-end reasoning process [20]. For example, feature importance scores, model confidence levels, and domain-specific thresholds can be combined into a NLP explanation that contextualises the model's output within the problem domain.

LLMs also enable user-adaptive explanations, addressing one of the long-standing challenges in interpretability: the diversity of explanation needs. Different users require different levels of abstraction and technical detail. A domain expert may seek explanations grounded in quantitative relationships and model sensitivity, while a decision-maker or stakeholder may require high-level justifications and implications. LLMs can dynamically adjust explanations based on the user's role, expertise, or preferences, thereby supporting personalised interpretability without modifying the underlying predictive model [21].

Another important role of LLMs is their capacity to support interactive and exploratory interpretability. Traditional post-hoc explanation methods typically produce static outputs, such as saliency maps or feature rankings [22]. In contrast, LLM-based systems allow users to engage in a dialogue with the model, asking follow-up questions such as "What would have changed the outcome?" "Which variables were most influential in this specific case?", or "How does this result compare to previous observations?". This interactive paradigm transforms interpretability from a one-way explanation into a collaborative reasoning process, where users actively probe and refine their understanding of the system [23].

LLMs also facilitate context-aware explanations, which are particularly valuable in complex, domain-specific applications. In areas such as environmental monitoring, healthcare, or policy analysis, raw model explanations may lack meaning unless they are grounded in domain knowledge [24]. LLMs can incorporate external context, such as regulatory standards, scientific guidelines, or historical trends, to frame model outputs in a meaningful, actionable way. For instance, a predicted water quality class can be explained in relation to established environmental thresholds, seasonal patterns, or known ecological risks, making the explanation more informative than a numerical score alone [25].

However, using LLMs for interpretability introduces new challenges and limitations. LLM-generated explanations are not guaranteed to faithfully represent the true internal reasoning of the underlying model [26]. Since LLMs generate explanations based on learned linguistic patterns rather than direct access to model internals, there is a risk of producing explanations that are plausible but inaccurate. This phenomenon, sometimes referred to as explanation hallucination, highlights the importance of grounding LLM explanations in verifiable model outputs, such as feature attributions, uncertainty estimates, or rule-based constraints. As a result, LLMs should be viewed as facilitators of interpretability rather than standalone explanation engines [27].

Recent research increasingly explores hybrid interpretability frameworks, in which classical XAI methods provide faithful, low-level signals, and LLMs operate on these signals to generate structured, coherent, and user-friendly explanations [28]. In such architectures, LLMs do not replace traditional interpretability techniques; instead, they act as reasoning layers that synthesise and communicate their outputs. This approach preserves explanation fidelity while leveraging LLMs' communicative strengths.

Finally, the integration of LLMs into interpretability reflects a broader shift in AI system design, from isolated models toward agentic and human-centred AI systems. In these systems, interpretability is no longer an optional add-on but an integral component of the decision-making pipeline. LLMs enable AI systems to justify, critique, and contextualise their own outputs, supporting transparency, accountability, and trust. This evolution positions LLM-based interpretability as a key enabler for deploying complex AI systems in real-world, high-stakes environments, setting the foundation for the agentic interpretability mechanisms discussed in the subsequent sections of this chapter.

## 4.3  Interpretability Mechanisms Within Agentic Architectures

As AI systems evolve from monolithic models toward agentic architectures, interpretability must also evolve from isolated explanation techniques to system-level and interaction-level transparency. Agentic AI systems are composed of multiple autonomous or semi-autonomous agents that perceive, reason, act, and communicate with one another. While this design enables scalability, flexibility, and task specialisation, it also introduces interpretability challenges that cannot be addressed by model-centric explanation methods alone [29].

Traditional Multi-Agent Systems (MAS) were originally developed in symbolic or rule-based settings, where agents followed predefined protocols, decision rules, or optimisation strategies. In these systems, interpretability was often implicit: agent behaviour could be inspected through rules, state transitions, or utility functions. However, classical MAS architectures were not designed to integrate data-driven models or NLP reasoning [30]. As a result, when interpretability or explanation was required, it was typically implemented externally, through logging mechanisms, post-hoc analysis, or separate explanation modules detached from the agents' reasoning processes.

When modern DL models were later incorporated into traditional MAS, this separation became even more pronounced. Neural models operated as opaque components inside agents, while explanations were generated outside the system, often without direct access to intermediate reasoning states. This architectural disconnect limited MAS's ability to produce coherent, user-oriented explanations, making interpretability an afterthought rather than an integral capability of the system [31].

In contrast, Agentic AI architectures are explicitly designed to integrate LLMs as first-class components of the system. In these architectures, LLMs are not merely external explanation tools but act as reasoning, coordination, and interpretation engines within agents themselves. This native integration enables agents to directly operate on structured and unstructured information, reason over intermediate results, and generate explanations as part of their decision-making process [32]. As a result, interpretability becomes embedded in the system's operational flow rather than appended post hoc.

A key advantage of Agentic AI's interpretability lies in its tight coupling of perception, reasoning, and explanation [33]. Agents can receive raw inputs, intermediate model outputs, and contextual metadata, and use LLMs to synthesise explanations that reflect the actual information processed by the system. This allows explanations to be grounded in real agent states, messages, and decisions, reducing the gap between system behaviour and user-facing interpretation [34].

Furthermore, agentic architectures support explainability through interaction. Unlike traditional MAS, where explanations are typically static or predefined, Agentic AI systems enable dynamic, conversational interpretability [35]. Users can query agents about specific decisions, request alternative explanations, or explore counterfactual scenarios. Because LLMs are embedded within the agents, these explanations can be generated on demand, conditioned on both system state and user intent [36].

Another important distinction lies in how information flows through the system. In classical MAS, inter-agent communication is often limited to structured messages or symbolic representations, which are not directly interpretable by humans. In agentic systems, communication can be augmented or mediated by LLMs, enabling agents to produce both machine-readable and human-readable representations of their internal reasoning [37]. This dual-channel communication supports trace-based interpretability, enabling the reconstruction of a decision's evolution from agent interactions.

Despite these strengths, agentic interpretability also introduces new challenges. The flexibility of LLM-based reasoning increases the risk of explanations that are persuasive but not fully faithful to the underlying computations. To address this, agentic architectures increasingly rely on grounded interpretability mechanisms, such as constrained prompts, access to verifiable agent logs, and hybrid pipelines that combine symbolic traces with data-driven explanations [32]. These safeguards help ensure that interpretability remains accurate, auditable, and aligned with system behaviour.

Overall, the transition from traditional MAS to Agentic AI represents a fundamental shift in how interpretability is conceived and implemented. Rather than treating explanations as external artefacts, agentic architectures integrate interpretability directly into the agents' reasoning processes. This enables AI systems not only to make decisions but also to understand, justify, and communicate those decisions in ways meaningful to human users. In doing so, Agentic AI provides a scalable and human-centred framework for interpretability that aligns with the increasing complexity and autonomy of modern AI systems.

# References


1. Yu Zhang et al. "A Survey on Neural Network Interpretability". In: *IEEE Transactions on Emerging Topics in Computational Intelligence* 5.5 (2021), pp. 726–742. DOI: https://doi.org/10.1109/TETCI.2021.3100641.
2. Feng-Lei Fan et al. "On Interpretability of Artificial Neural Networks: A Survey". In: *IEEE Transactions on Radiation and Plasma Medical Sciences* 5.6 (2021), pp. 741–760. DOI: https://doi.org/10.1109/TRPMS.2021.3066428.
3. Christoph Molnar, Giuseppe Casalicchio, and Bernd Bischl. "Interpretable Machine Learning – A Brief History, State-of-the-Art and Challenges". In: *ECML PKDD 2020 Workshops*. Ed. by Irena Koprinska et al. Cham: Springer International Publishing, 2020, pp. 417–431. DOI: https://doi.org/10.1007/978-3-030-65965-3_28.
4. Rudresh Dwivedi et al. "Explainable AI (XAI): Core ideas, techniques, and solutions". In: *ACM computing surveys* 55.9 (2023), pp. 1–33. DOI: https://doi.org/10.1145/3561048.
5. Chaobo Zhang et al. "Intrinsically interpretable machine learning-based building energy load prediction method with high accuracy and strong interpretability". In: *Energy and Built Environment* (2024). ISSN: 2666-1233. DOI: https://doi.org/10.1016/j.enbenv.2024.08.006.
6. Sven Kruschel et al. "Challenging the performance-interpretability trade-off: an evaluation of interpretable machine learning models". In: *Business & Information Systems Engineering* (2025), pp. 1–25. DOI: https://doi.org/10.1007/s12599-024-00922-2.
7. Andreas Madsen, Siva Reddy, and Sarath Chandar. "Post-hoc interpretability for neural nlp: A survey". In: *ACM Computing Surveys* 55.8 (2022), pp. 1–42. DOI: https://doi.org/10.1145/3546577.
8. Carla Piazzon Vieira and Luciano Antonio Digiampietri. "Machine Learning post-hoc interpretability: a systematic mapping study". In: *Proceedings of the XVIII Brazilian Symposium on Information Systems*. SBSI '22. Curitiba, Brazil: Association for Computing Machinery, 2022. ISBN: 9781450396981. DOI: https://doi.org/10.1145/3535511.3535512.
9. Sungsoo Ray Hong, Jessica Hullman, and Enrico Bertini. "Human Factors in Model Interpretability: Industry Practices, Challenges, and Needs". In: *Proc. ACM Hum.-Comput. Interact.* 4.CSCW1 (May 2020). DOI: https://doi.org/10.1145/3392878.
10. Lynda Dib and Laurence Capus. "Classifying XAI Methods to Resolve Conceptual Ambiguity". In: *Technologies* 13.9 (2025). ISSN: 2227-7080. DOI: https://doi.org/10.3390/technologies13090390.
11. Ettore Mariotti, José María Alonso Moral, and Albert Gatt. "Exploring the balance between interpretability and performance with carefully designed constrainable Neural Additive Models". In: *Information Fusion* 99 (2023), p. 101882. ISSN: 1566-2535. DOI: https://doi.org/10.1016/j.inffus.2023.101882.
12. Chaofan Chen et al. "A holistic approach to interpretability in financial lending: Models, visualizations, and summary-explanations". In: *Decision Support Systems* 152 (2022), p. 113647. ISSN: 0167-9236. DOI: https://doi.org/10.1016/j.dss.2021.113647.
13. Qiaoying Teng et al. "A survey on the interpretability of deep learning in medical diagnosis". In: *Multimedia Systems* 28.6 (2022), pp. 2335–2355. DOI: https://doi.org/10.1007/s00530-022-00960-4.
14. Yunkai Dang et al. *Explainable and Interpretable Multimodal Large Language Models: A Comprehensive Survey*. 2024. DOI: https://doi.org/10.48550/arXiv.2412.02104. arXiv: 2412.02104 `[cs.CL]`.
15. Inès Arous et al. "Llm explainability". In: *Handbook of Human-Centered Artificial Intelligence*. Springer, 2025, pp. 1–61. DOI: https://doi.org/10.1007/978-981-97-8440-0_85-1.
16. Razi Iqbal and Nathan Stuart Hamill. "Interpretable SLM-Driven Trust Framework for Smart Cities: Managing Distributed Energy Resources in Networked Microgrids". In: *Smart Cities* 8.6 (2025). ISSN: 2624-6511. DOI: https://doi.org/10.3390/smartcities8060186.
17. Graham M Jones, Shai Satran, and Arvind Satyanarayan. "Toward cultural interpretability: A linguistic anthropological framework for describing and evaluating large language models".

In: *Big Data & Society* 12.1 (2025), p. 20539517241303118. DOI: https://doi.org/10.1177/20539517241303118.

18. Qianli Wang et al. "LLMCheckup: Conversational Examination of Large Language Models via Interpretability Tools and Self-Explanations". In: *Proceedings of the Third Workshop on Bridging Human–Computer Interaction and Natural Language Processing*. Ed. by Su Lin Blodgett et al. Mexico City, Mexico: Association for Computational Linguistics, June 2024, pp. 89–104. DOI: https://doi.org/10.18653/v1/2024.hcinlp-1.9.

19. Jingyuan Yang et al. "Enhancing Semantic Consistency of Large Language Models through Model Editing: An Interpretability-Oriented Approach". In: *Findings of the Association for Computational Linguistics: ACL 2024*. Ed. by Lun-Wei Ku, Andre Martins, and Vivek Srikumar. Bangkok, Thailand: Association for Computational Linguistics, Aug. 2024, pp. 3343–3353. DOI: https://doi.org/10.18653/v1/2024.findings-acl.199.

20. Xuansheng Wu et al. *Interpreting and Steering LLMs with Mutual Information-based Explanations on Sparse Autoencoders*. 2025. DOI: https://doi.org/10.48550/arXiv.2502.15576. arXiv: 2502.15576 [cs.CL].

21. Fuseini Mumuni and Alhassan Mumuni. *Explainable artificial intelligence (XAI): from inherent explainability to large language models*. 2025. DOI: https://doi.org/10.48550/arXiv.2501.09967. arXiv: 2501.09967 [cs.LG].

22. Miguel Fontes, João Dallyson Sousa De Almeida, and António Cunha. "Application of Example-Based Explainable Artificial Intelligence (XAI) for Analysis and Interpretation of Medical Imaging: A Systematic Review". In: *IEEE Access* 12 (2024), pp. 26419–26427. DOI: https://doi.org/10.1109/ACCESS.2024.3367606.

23. Cheonsu Jeong. "Design and Evaluation Methods for LLM-Based Explainable AI (XAI)-Based Human-AI Collaboration Systems". In: *Advances in Artificial Intelligence and Machine Learning* 5.3 (2025), p. 240. DOI: https://doi.org/10.54364/AAIML.2025.53240.

24. Yuhe Ji et al. "Adapting Large Language Models to Log Analysis with Interpretable Domain Knowledge". In: *Proceedings of the 34th ACM International Conference on Information and Knowledge Management*. CIKM '25. Seoul, Republic of Korea: Association for Computing Machinery, 2025, pp. 1135–1144. ISBN: 9798400720406. DOI: https://doi.org/10.1145/3746252.3761189.

25. Fei Wu et al. "Knowledge-Empowered, Collaborative, and Co-Evolving AI Models: The Post-LLM Roadmap". In: *Engineering* 44 (2025), pp. 87–100. ISSN: 2095-8099. DOI: https://doi.org/10.1016/j.eng.2024.12.008.

26. Chandan Singh et al. *Rethinking Interpretability in the Era of Large Language Models*. 2024. DOI: https://doi.org/10.48550/arXiv.2402.01761. arXiv: 2402.01761 [cs.CL].

27. I Papagiannopoulos et al. "Comparison of explainability methods for hallucination analysis in LLMs [version 1; peer review: 1 approved with reservations, 2 not approved]". In: *Open Research Europe* 5.191 (2025). DOI: https://doi.org/10.12688/openreseurope.20839.1.

28. Yulin Chen et al. "When interpretability meets noise: An LLM-assisted hybrid deep logical rule learning framework". In: *Machine Learning* 114.12 (2025), p. 283. DOI: https://doi.org/10.1007/s10994-025-06931-w.

29. Suruchi Deshmukh et al. "Agentic AI: A Survey of Autonomous Agents, Architectures, and Emerging Applications". In: *IEEE 5th International Conference on ICT in Business Industry & Government (ICTBIG)*. 2025, pp. 1–8. DOI: https://doi.org/10.1109/ICTBIG68706.2025.11323264.

30. Mert Cemri et al. *Why Do Multi-Agent LLM Systems Fail?*. 2025. DOI: https://doi.org/10.48550/arXiv.2503.13657. arXiv: 2503.13657 [cs.AI].

31. Clément Blanco-Volle et al. "Explainability and Interpretability of an Ensemble Multi-agent System for Supervised Learning". In: *International Conference on Principles and Practice of Multi-Agent Systems*. Springer. 2024, pp. 335–350. DOI: https://doi.org/10.1007/978-3-031-77367-9_26.

32. Jithesh Yemi Reddy. "Interpretability and Trust in Large Language and Agentic Models: A Survey of Methods, Metrics, and Applications". In: *Engrxiv* (2025). DOI: https://doi.org/10.31224/6090.

33. Pradipta Kishore Chakrabarty. "Causal Inference in Agentic AI: Bridging Explainability and Dynamic Decision Making". In: *International Journal of Science and Research (IJSR)* 14.4 (2025), pp. 10–21275. DOI: https://doi.org/10.21275/SR25424081718.

34. Lifu Huang et al. "Towards Agentic AI for Science: Hypothesis Generation, Comprehension, Quantification, and Validation". In: *Companion Proceedings of the ACM on Web Conference 2025*. WWW '25. Sydney NSW, Australia: Association for Computing Machinery, 2025, pp. 1639–1642. ISBN: 9798400713316. DOI: https://doi.org/10.1145/3701716.3717754.

35. Marine Pagliari, Valérian Chambon, and Bruno Berberian. "What is new with Artificial Intelligence? Human–agent interactions through the lens of social agency". In: *Frontiers in Psychology* Volume 13 - 2022 (2022). DOI: https://doi.org/10.3389/fpsyg.2022.954444.

36. Been Kim et al. *Because we have LLMs, we Can and Should Pursue Agentic Interpretability*. 2025. DOI: https://doi.org/10.48550/arXiv.2506.12152. arXiv: 2506.12152 [cs.AI].

37. Alex Grzankowski. "Real sparks of artificial intelligence and the importance of inner interpretability". In: *Inquiry* 0.0 (2024), pp. 1–27. DOI: https://doi.org/10.1080/0020174X.2023.2296468.

# Chapter 5
# Learning and Adaptation in Agentic AI

**Abstract** This chapter explores the learning mechanisms that enable Agentic Artificial Intelligence (AI) systems to adapt over time in dynamic environments. It focuses on Reinforcement Learning (RL) and multi-agent learning frameworks that support continuous policy refinement through interaction and feedback. The chapter examines challenges such as non-stationarity, coordination stability, and credit assignment in multi-agent settings. Learning is framed as an ongoing process operating across multiple temporal scales, enabling agents to balance short-term performance with long-term objectives. The integration of learning with language-based reasoning and coordination is discussed as a means of enhancing adaptability and resilience.

## 5.1 Reinforcement Learning

Learning dynamics is the theoretical study of how an algorithm's internal state, its parameters, its representations, and, in the case of decision systems, its policies, evolve under the combined influence of data, objective functions and optimisation procedures. From this perspective, learning is a trajectory in a high-dimensional state space, where initial conditions, algorithmic choices, and data statistics determine which regions of that space are visited, which attractors or states the system approaches, and how sensitive those outcomes are to perturbations. The study of learning dynamics seeks to explain transient behaviour and correct outcomes, to characterise stability, such as generalisation, robustness, and adaptability [1].

In the supervised paradigm, the theoretical focus is empirical risk minimisation and the interaction between optimisation trajectories and model complexity. Here, the focus is on applying input data and supervising the outcomes through a target feature. This target feature helps the AI algorithm determine whether the result was correct. The algorithm then adjusts the associated metrics to reflect whether the trained model achieved an overall good performance. Therefore, key questions appear, such as how different optimisation algorithms bias parameter trajectories toward solutions with particular properties, and how internal representations of features emerge and stabilise during training [2]. Theoretical tools used here include



P. Oliveira et al., *Architectures for Agentic AI*, SpringerBriefs in Intelligent Systems,
https://doi.org/10.1007/978-3-032-24781-0_5

convergence results from optimisation theory, linearised or mean-field approximations that render the dynamics tractable in specific regimes, and capacity measures from statistical learning theory that relate the properties of learned functions and the algorithm's implicit biases to sample complexity. Dynamical analyses often examine the spectral properties of curvature and the time evolution of representation statistics to explain effects such as early learning of certain features and late refinement of others [3].

Unsupervised learning is theoretically more subtle because no external target feature signal drives the updates. Instead, objectives seek to capture the statistical structure of the inputs, whether by compressing observations, modelling their density, or maximising functional predictive or contrastive objectives. In simple linear settings, iterative algorithms admit closed-form dynamical descriptions and convergence guarantees; in nonlinear settings, theory often relies on information-theoretic and geometric assumptions about the data manifold [4]. Transposing this into practical terms means finding intricate relationships among the data. Still, instead of receiving a result, the outcome will be to export it to a three-dimensional space, where each representation is a vector. It can then be used to find the nearest one to determine whether they are similar, or to create clusters of classes that they can characterise [5].

Learning dynamics, therefore, sets the stage for studying particular learning paradigms through a dynamical lens. Each paradigm specifies a different objective, source of information, and constraints on how updates reshape the learner's trajectory. RL exemplifies the richest dynamical behaviour because the learner's actions actively shape future data and feedback [1]. In what follows, the chapter narrows from the general theory of learning dynamics to a focused theoretical treatment of RL, examining the unique sources of non-stationarity, the mechanisms of temporal reward assignment, and the conceptual challenges that arise when function approximation, exploration, and sequential dependence are combined.

RL is the paradigm in which learning dynamics are most tightly coupled to the evolution of the learner's environment. Conceptually, a reinforcement learner, also called an agent, chooses actions in a sequence of interactions and receives scalar feedback that evaluates those actions [6]. These actions influence which observations and rewards occur next, with rewards received from environments in which the agent has performed the action. The data distribution is endogenous: updates to the learner change the future training signal, creating a closed feedback loop between policy updates and experience statistics [7].

A core theoretical concept is temporal credit assignment, in which rewards indicate to the RL agent whether the performed action was appropriate. The reward system is either positive or negative. The first allows the agent to learn that the performed action was good, thereby adjusting its algorithm accordingly, while the second ensures that the action was not suitable, thereby adapting the algorithm to avoid such actions. This problem interacts with function approximation and stochastic updates to determine whether learning converges to a stable solution or enters oscillatory or divergent regimes, which are essential for ensuring that the agent achieves its objective [8].

In addition, when the environment rewards the agent, it also sends the agent's state. This allows the agent to know the environment's condition.

Exploration versus exploitation defines another central class of dynamical questions. A learner must gain practical experience while leveraging current knowledge to achieve performance. Theoretical formulations of exploration usually take the form of regret or sample-complexity bounds in stylised environments; these bounds characterise the minimal amount of exploration required to guarantee near-optimal behaviour [3]. Extending these guarantees beyond small or structured environments to high-dimensional settings with expressive function approximators remains open. From a dynamic point of view, exploration mechanisms shape early trajectories: they determine which regions of state space are visited, which local minima are seen, and what representation structure can form.

The bias–variance trade-offs of gradient and value estimates also control stability. Policy updates derived from noisy, high-variance gradient estimates can destabilise learning unless variance is controlled or updates are regularised. In actor–critic learning, the critic's inaccuracies influence the actor's updates, coupling two learning processes whose combined dynamics may admit fixed points, limit cycles, or chaotic behaviour, depending on the architecture, timescale separation, and update rules. Theoretical analyses, therefore, often focus on how error propagates through these coupled systems and on the conditions under which timescale separation or smoothing restores stability [2].

These fundamental concerns regarding stability and error propagation are architecturally codified in the distinction between model-free and model-based reinforcement learning. The choice of whether to explicitly learn a model of the environment's dynamics determines the specific dynamical regime the agent instantiates. While model-free methods grapple with the variance of direct experience, learning an internal model changes the problem to one with an internal planning loop: the agent's dynamics now encompass the learned model's dynamics and the planner's behaviour. Theoretical work on model-based approaches, therefore, studies how model error amplifies during planning and how the distribution of imagined trajectories affects policy updates [9]. These factors alter sample efficiency and stability, as reflected in the parameter trajectory and the evolving representation of dynamics and value.

Representation learning within RL deserves particular theoretical attention. Good representations can dramatically alter learning trajectories by improving generalisation across states, reducing variance of value estimates, and enabling more efficient credit assignment [10]. Theoretically, representation learning is analysed in terms of sufficiency and compactness: representations that preserve the information needed for optimal decisions while discarding irrelevant variation yield simpler downstream dynamics [11]. How such representations are induced by intrinsic objectives, auxiliary predictions, or particular update rules is an active theoretical topic.

Multi-agent settings introduce an additional layer of dynamical complexity: each learner's updates change the environment for the others. The resulting coupled system can be studied through equilibrium concepts and stability analyses borrowed from game theory and dynamical systems. Questions include the existence and stability of equilibria, the learning dynamics under best-response updates, and the emergence of cooperative or adversarial structures as properties of the joint dynamical system [12].

From a theoretical methods perspective, several analytical tools are central to the study of RL dynamics. Dynamical systems theory provides language for fixed points, attractors, stability and bifurcations as hyperparameters vary. Stochastic process approximations model the effect of sampling noise on update trajectories and characterise escape times from basins. Statistical learning theory provides a framework for relating approximation capacity and complexity to sample complexity and generalisation guarantees [13]. Mean-field and limit approximations sometimes render high-dimensional dynamics tractable by identifying regimes where behaviour simplifies. Control-theoretic ideas contribute notions of robustness and closed-loop stability that are particularly relevant when learning and control must be integrated [14].

Important theoretical observables are convergence rates of policy and value estimates, sample complexity measured in interactions to achieve near-optimal performance, regret in online settings, and the spectral and stability properties of linearisations around learned solutions. There are persistent open problems: producing non-vacuous, optimiser-aware generalisation guarantees for rich function approximations; proving convergence guarantees for RL methods with expressive models in continuous domains; and unifying the various analytical tools into a coherent account that predicts when and why specific algorithmic scaffolds (such as smoothing, target stabilisation, or constrained updates) restore stable dynamics [1].

## 5.2  Coordinated Learning in Multi-agent Environments

RL within agentic architectures extends classical learning dynamics by embedding learning agents into systems composed of multiple interacting decision-making entities. In this setting, learning is no longer confined to a single policy that optimises a fixed objective in a stationary environment. Instead, learning dynamics unfold across layers of interaction, communication, coordination, and adaptation, where each agent's learning process contributes to shaping the effective environment experienced by others [15]. This shift transforms RL from an isolated optimisation problem into a distributed, co-evolving dynamical system.

In these architectures, RL operates at multiple levels of abstraction. At the individual level, an agent may learn a policy that maps observations to actions, optimising a local reward signal. At the system level, however, collective behaviour emerges from the interactions among multiple learning processes, each governed by its own objectives, representations, and update rules. The global learning dynamics, therefore, cannot be reduced to the convergence properties of any single agent. Instead, they arise from the coupling of learning trajectories through communication channels, shared resources, and interdependent reward structures [16].

One of the defining characteristics of RL in agentic systems is endogenous non-stationarity. Unlike classical single-agent settings, where non-stationarity typically arises from exploration noise or changing environments, agentic systems introduce structural non-stationarity through learning itself [17]. As agents update their policies, they modify the statistical properties of the environment observed by other agents. This feedback loop creates learning dynamics that may exhibit oscillations, phase transitions, or transient coordination regimes before stabilising. Understanding and controlling this non-stationarity is a central theoretical challenge in agentic RL [18].

When moving over to communication, it plays a critical role in shaping learning dynamics within agentic architectures. Messages exchanged between agents are not merely coordination signals; they can function as learned abstractions that compress state information, convey intent, or shape reward expectations. From a dynamical perspective, communication introduces additional state variables into the learning process, expanding the effective state space [19]. Learning to communicate, or learning through communication, therefore becomes an intertwined optimisation problem, where agents must adapt both their action policies and their communicative behaviour [20]. This coupling can accelerate convergence through shared information, but it can also destabilise learning if communication protocols drift or misalign.

Through inter-agent communications, the reward design and decomposition further differentiate agentic RL from classical formulations. In many agentic systems, agents are assigned local reward functions that reflect specialised objectives, while the system as a whole seeks to optimise a global goal. The relationship between local and global rewards determines whether learning dynamics encourage cooperation, competition, or mixed equilibria. Poorly aligned rewards can lead to pathological dynamics, such as agents optimising locally while degrading global performance [15]. Conversely, well-designed reward shaping and shared incentives can stabilise learning by creating attractors corresponding to cooperative equilibria.

Temporal credit assignment becomes more complex in agentic architectures because outcomes often depend on sequences of inter-agent interactions rather than isolated actions [8]. An agent's contribution to a global outcome may be indirect, delayed, or mediated by other agents' responses. Theoretical approaches to this problem include different reward functions, counterfactual baselines, and decentralised value decomposition, all of which aim to isolate an agent's marginal impact on collective performance [21]. These mechanisms reshape learning dynamics by reducing variance and clarifying the causal structure of rewards, thereby enabling more stable and efficient learning trajectories.

Another important dimension concerns the separation of learning timescales across agents. In practical agentic architectures, different agents may learn at different rates or operate with different update frequencies [22]. Some agents may adapt rapidly to short-term feedback, while others evolve slowly to provide stability or long-term memory. From a dynamical systems perspective, this timescale separation can stabilise learning by preventing fast oscillations, but it can also introduce delayed feedback effects that complicate convergence analysis [23]. Understanding how to balance these timescales is crucial for designing robust agentic learning systems.

Function approximation further amplifies the complexity of learning dynamics in agentic RL. When agents employ deep neural networks or Large Language Models (LLM)-based policies, their internal representations evolve alongside their policies. These representations influence not only action selection but also communication, message interpretation, and reward estimation [24]. As a result, learning dynamics unfold jointly in policy space and representation space, creating rich trajectories that may exhibit sudden shifts as internal abstractions reorganise. Theoretical analysis of such systems often relies on approximations that separate representation learning from policy learning, though this separation is only partially valid in practice.

The integration of LLMs into agentic architectures introduces additional layers to RL dynamics. LLM-enabled agents may not learn policies solely through numerical updates but also through linguistic feedback, evaluative prompts, or structured critique generated by other agents [25]. In this setting, reinforcement signals can be symbolic or semantic rather than purely scalar. Learning dynamics, therefore, include the evolution of explanation quality, reasoning coherence, and communicative effectiveness, extending RL beyond traditional control objectives into the space of interpretability and interaction.

Multi-Agent Reinforcement Learning (MARL) theory provides partial tools for analysing these dynamics, borrowing concepts from game theory, evolutionary dynamics, and control theory. Equilibrium concepts such as Nash equilibria or correlated equilibria offer static characterisations of possible outcomes, but they often fail to capture transient learning behaviour or path dependence [12]. Dynamical systems analyses, by contrast, emphasise how learning unfolds over time, identifying conditions under which cooperative behaviour emerges, collapses, or cycles. These analyses highlight that stability in agentic RL is not guaranteed by optimality alone but depends critically on algorithmic choices, communication structures, and reward alignment [26].

On the whole, RL within agentic architectures represents a qualitative expansion of classical learning dynamics. Learning is no longer a solitary trajectory toward an optimum but a collective process shaped by interaction, communication, and adaptation. This perspective reframes RL as a system-level phenomenon in which stability, efficiency, and interpretability emerge from the coordinated evolution of multiple learning agents. This framework sets the foundation for the subsequent sections, which examine how RL is specialised through domain-specific fine-tuning, evaluated at the system level, and ultimately instantiated in the multi-agent case study presented in this work.

## 5.3   Domain-Specific Fine-Tuning through Reinforcement Learning

Domain-specific fine-tuning through RL represents a critical stage in the learning dynamics of modern AI systems. While pre-trained models and general-purpose learning algorithms provide broad competence across tasks, they rarely capture the nuanced objectives, constraints, and evaluation criteria of specialised domains [27]. RL offers a principled mechanism for aligning system behaviour with domain-specific goals by shaping learning trajectories through carefully designed reward signals and interaction structures.

From a learning dynamics perspective, domain-specific fine-tuning can be understood as a controlled deformation of an existing policy or representation. Rather than learning from scratch, the system begins from a pre-trained or pre-optimised state and is guided toward a region of parameter space that reflects domain-relevant performance criteria [28]. This process reshapes both the policy landscape and the model's internal representations, often producing behaviours that would not emerge under generic optimisation objectives alone.

Historically, policy-gradient methods have played a central role in enabling stable RL for complex function approximators. Early approaches suffered from instability caused by large or poorly controlled updates, often leading to catastrophic performance degradation. This motivated the development of trust-region methods, which explicitly constrained policy updates to remain within a bounded region of the current policy. Proximal Policy Optimisation (PPO) emerged as a practical and computationally efficient approximation of these trust-region ideas. By clipping policy updates or penalising divergence from the previous policy, PPO stabilised learning dynamics while retaining the flexibility required for high-dimensional and continuous control tasks [29].

PPO's conceptual contribution lies in its balance between adaptability and stability. It allows policies to improve incrementally while preventing abrupt shifts that could destabilise learning [30]. This property made PPO particularly influential in domains where feedback is noisy, delayed, or partially subjective, such as robotics, game playing, and, later, Natural Language Processing (NLP) generation. PPO established a foundation for reliably applying RL to large neural models, including early language models fine-tuned for alignment and preference optimisation [31].

As RL began to be applied to increasingly expressive models and more abstract objectives, such as explanation quality, coherence, and alignment with human preferences, new challenges emerged. In these settings, rewards are often derived from learned evaluators or comparative judgements rather than explicit environmental signals. This shift motivated the development of more generalised policy optimisation frameworks, including Group Relative Policy Optimisation (GRPO). GRPO extends the stabilisation principles of PPO by incorporating relative, group-based evaluation signals, enabling policies to be optimised based on comparative performance across candidate outputs rather than absolute scalar rewards [32].

From a conceptual standpoint, GRPO represents an evolution of PPO rather than a departure from it. While PPO constrains updates relative to a single previous policy, GRPO operates over distributions of candidate behaviours, using relative assessments to guide learning. This makes GRPO particularly well-suited for domains where quality is inherently comparative, such as NLP explanations, reasoning traces, or interpretability outputs [31]. In such contexts, absolute notions of correctness may be ill-defined, whereas relative preference provides a more stable and informative learning signal.

Domain-specific RL relies on carefully constructed reward functions that encode expert knowledge, operational priorities, and contextual constraints. Unlike generic benchmarks, domain rewards often reflect composite objectives that combine accuracy, consistency, interpretability, safety, and adherence to external standards [33]. Theoretical work shows that poorly specified rewards can induce unintended attractors, where the learner optimises proxy objectives at the expense of true domain goals. PPO and its successors mitigate some of these risks by limiting policy drift, while GRPO additionally leverages comparative evaluation to stabilise learning in ambiguous reward landscapes [32].

Fine-tuning through RL also introduces domain-aware challenges in credit assignment. In complex decision pipelines, particularly those involving explanations or multi-stage reasoning, the quality of an outcome may depend on multiple intermediate choices. RL enables the propagation of evaluative signals backwards through these decision chains, allowing the system to adjust not only final outputs but also intermediate reasoning steps [34]. PPO-style stabilisation ensures that these adjustments occur gradually, while GRPO's relative evaluation allows learning to focus on improving distinctions between alternative behaviours.

When applied to systems incorporating LLMs, domain-specific RL extends beyond numerical optimisation to linguistic and semantic alignment. LLMs fine-tuned through RL are encouraged to generate responses that satisfy domain-specific norms, terminologies, and explanatory standards. PPO laid the groundwork for this paradigm by enabling stable language model fine-tuning, while GRPO further refines it by optimising over sets of generated explanations evaluated relative to one another [32]. In this sense, RL becomes a mechanism for shaping communicative and interpretive behaviour, not merely task performance.

In agentic architectures, domain-specific fine-tuning often occurs simultaneously across multiple levels. Individual agents may be fine-tuned to optimise specialised sub-objectives, while higher-level agents or evaluators assess global system behaviour [21]. Reinforcement signals can be distributed across agents, enabling coordinated adaptation where local improvements contribute to overall system alignment [24]. GRPO naturally supports this structure by allowing group-level evaluation across agents or outputs, reinforcing collective learning dynamics.

An important consideration in domain-specific RL is the balance between adaptation and stability. Excessive fine-tuning can lead to over-specialisation, reducing robustness and generalisation outside the training distribution [27]. Conversely, insufficient fine-tuning may underrepresent domain requirements. Learning dynamics theory emphasises the role of constrained updates, relative evaluation, and controlled learning rates in maintaining stability while allowing meaningful adaptation. PPO and GRPO exemplify this progression, each introducing mechanisms to preserve learning stability as objectives grow more abstract and domain-specific [30].

Overall, domain-specific fine-tuning through RL illustrates how general optimisation principles evolve to meet the demands of complex, real-world domains. The progression from PPO to GRPO reflects a broader trajectory in RL: from stabilising low-level control to aligning high-level reasoning and explanation with human and domain expectations. In agentic systems, this fine-tuning is not a terminal step but an ongoing process, allowing agents to continuously refine both their decisions and their explanations as domain conditions and evaluation criteria evolve.

## 5.4  Evaluating Agentic Learning

Evaluating learning in agentic systems requires a conceptual shift from traditional model-centric assessment toward system-level, process-oriented evaluation. In classical ML, evaluation is typically framed in terms of static performance metrics, such as accuracy, loss, or error rates measured on held-out data. While these metrics remain important, they are insufficient for agentic architectures in which learning unfolds over time, spans multiple interacting components, and influences both decision-making and explanatory behaviour. Agentic learning must therefore be evaluated not only by what the system achieves, but also by how it learns, adapts, and coordinates [16].

A defining challenge in evaluating agentic learning is its inherently dynamic nature. Learning trajectories in agentic systems evolve through continuous interaction with environments, other agents, and evaluative mechanisms. Policies, representations, and communication patterns change as feedback is incorporated, often in non-linear and path-dependent ways [35]. As a result, evaluation cannot be limited to final outcomes; it must also account for convergence behaviour, stability, and responsiveness to feedback. From a learning dynamics perspective, important questions include whether learning converges to stable regimes, whether oscillatory or divergent behaviours emerge, and how sensitive the system is to changes in reward structure, environment, or agent configuration.

Another key dimension of evaluation concerns multi-objective performance. Agentic systems typically optimise several, often competing, objectives simultaneously. In the context of interpretability-driven systems, these objectives may include predictive accuracy, explanation quality, coherence, consistency, domain alignment, and computational efficiency [36]. RL agents may improve performance along one dimension while degrading performance in another, making single-scalar metrics inadequate. Evaluating agentic learning, therefore, requires multi-dimensional assessment frameworks that capture trade-offs and interactions between objectives over time.

Evaluation in agentic systems must also address credit assignment at the system level. In multi-agent settings, improvements or failures are rarely attributable to a single component. Learning outcomes emerge from the interaction of agents, their communication patterns, and their coordinated adaptation. This complicates attribution: determining which agent or learning mechanism contributed to a particular outcome becomes a non-trivial problem [8]. Conceptually, this mirrors the credit assignment problem in RL, but extended to agent populations and interaction protocols. Effective evaluation frameworks must therefore consider both local agent-level learning signals and global system-level performance indicators.

Stability and robustness constitute another central evaluation criterion. Agentic learning systems operate in environments that may change over time, exhibit noise, or contain adversarial elements [16]. Evaluation must assess not only average performance but also resilience to perturbations, such as changes in input distribution, partial-agent failures, or inconsistent feedback. From a theoretical standpoint, robustness can be studied through sensitivity analysis of learning trajectories and by examining the system's ability to recover from suboptimal states [15]. Stable learning dynamics are particularly important in RL contexts, where poorly controlled updates can lead to catastrophic forgetting or policy collapse.

Interpretability introduces additional evaluation challenges unique to agentic systems. When learning involves optimising explanations, evaluation must consider both the quality of the explanations and their faithfulness to the underlying decision processes. Unlike traditional performance metrics, explanation quality is often subjective, context-dependent, and difficult to quantify [35]. Agentic learning frameworks increasingly rely on hybrid evaluation strategies that combine automated metrics, comparative assessments, and human-in-the-loop judgements. These approaches reflect the recognition that interpretability is not a purely technical property but a relational one, defined by the interaction between system outputs and human understanding [37].

Temporal evaluation plays a crucial role in assessing agentic learning. Because agentic systems operate continuously, evaluation must track how performance and behaviour evolve across learning episodes [1]. Learning curves, adaptation speed, and responsiveness to new feedback provide insight into whether learning mechanisms are effective and sustainable [6]. In RL settings, this includes analysing sample efficiency, convergence rates, and regret over time. In agentic architectures, temporal evaluation extends further to include the evolution of communication patterns, role specialisation, and emergent coordination strategies [21].

Another important evaluative dimension is alignment with domain and human expectations. Agentic learning systems often operate in applied settings where correctness alone is insufficient; outputs must conform to domain standards, ethical constraints, and user expectations [33]. Evaluation, therefore, includes assessing whether learned behaviours remain within acceptable operational boundaries. RL fine-tuning methods, such as PPO and GRPO, introduce mechanisms to constrain learning updates, but their effectiveness must be empirically and conceptually evaluated to ensure that optimisation does not exploit unintended reward loopholes [30].

Scalability and generalisation also feature prominently in evaluating agentic learning. As the number of agents, tasks, or environmental complexity increases, evaluation must determine whether learning mechanisms continue to function effectively. This includes assessing whether coordination overhead grows unmanageably, whether learning signals remain informative, and whether emergent behaviours remain interpretable. Generalisation, in this context, refers not only to performance on unseen data but also to the system's ability to adapt to new tasks, domains, or interaction patterns without extensive retraining [21].

Finally, evaluating agentic learning involves methodological considerations about what constitutes evidence of successful learning. Because agentic systems are complex and often non-deterministic, evaluation results may vary across runs, initial conditions, and random seeds. This variability necessitates statistical evaluation protocols that account for uncertainty and variance in learning outcomes. It also motivates qualitative analysis of agent behaviour, communication traces, and decision rationales, complementing quantitative metrics with interpretive insight.

In summary, evaluating agentic learning requires a holistic, multi-level approach that reflects the complexity of agentic architectures and RL dynamics. Effective evaluation must consider not only final performance but also learning trajectories, stability, robustness, coordination, interpretability, and alignment. By adopting this broader evaluative lens, researchers and practitioners can better understand how agentic systems learn, when they succeed, and where their limitations lie. This perspective is essential for deploying agentic AI systems in real-world domains where sustained autonomy, trust, and adaptability are as important as raw performance.

# References


1. Ashish Kumar Shakya, Gopinatha Pillai, and Sohom Chakrabarty. "Reinforcement learning algorithms: A brief survey". In: *Expert Systems with Applications* 231 (2023), p. 120495. ISSN: 0957-4174. DOI: 10.1016/j.eswa.2023.120495.
2. Yunhao Tang. "Biased Gradient Estimate with Drastic Variance Reduction for Meta Reinforcement Learning". In: *Proceedings of the 39th International Conference on Machine Learning*. Ed. by Kamalika Chaudhuri et al. Vol. 162. Proceedings of Machine Learning Research. PMLR, 2022, pp. 21050–21075. DOI: 10.48550/arXiv.2112.07328.
3. Robert C Wilson et al. "Balancing exploration and exploitation with information and randomization". In: *Current Opinion in Behavioral Sciences* 38 (2021). Computational cognitive neuroscience, pp. 49–56. ISSN: 2352-1546. DOI: 10.1016/j.cobeha.2020.10.001.
4. Chengchun Shi et al. "Statistical Inference of the Value Function for Reinforcement Learning in Infinite-Horizon Settings". In: *Journal of the Royal Statistical Society Series B: Statistical Methodology* 84.3 (Dec. 2021), pp. 765–793. ISSN: 1369-7412. DOI: 10.1111/rssb.12465.
5. Samreen Naeem et al. "An unsupervised machine learning algorithms: Comprehensive review". In: *International Journal of Computing and Digital Systems* (2023). DOI: 10.12785/ijcds/130172.
6. Sindhu Padakandla. "A Survey of Reinforcement Learning Algorithms for Dynamically Varying Environments". In: *ACM Comput. Surv.* 54.6 (July 2021). ISSN: 0360-0300. DOI: 10.1145/3459991.
7. Shengbo Eben Li. "Deep Reinforcement Learning". In: *Reinforcement Learning for Sequential Decision and Optimal Control*. Singapore: Springer Nature Singapore, 2023, pp. 365–402. ISBN: 978-981-19-7784-8. DOI: 10.1007/978-981-19-7784-8_10.
8. Dong Yan et al. "Deep reinforcement learning with credit assignment for combinatorial optimization". In: *Pattern Recognition* 124 (2022), p. 108466. ISSN: 0031-3203. DOI: 10.1016/j.patcog.2021.108466.
9. Thomas M. Moerland et al. "Model-based Reinforcement Learning: A Survey". In: *Foundations and Trends in Machine Learning* 16.1 (Jan. 2023), pp. 1–118. ISSN: 1935-8237. DOI: 10.1561/2200000086.

10. Nicolo̊Ł Botteghi, Mannes Poel, and Christoph Brune. "Unsupervised Representation Learning in Deep Reinforcement Learning: A Review". In: *IEEE Control Systems* 45.2 (2025), pp. 26–68. DOI: 10.1109/MCS.2025.3534477.

11. Denis Yarats et al. "Reinforcement Learning with Prototypical Representations". In: *Proceedings of the 38th International Conference on Machine Learning*. Ed. by Marina Meila and Tong Zhang. Vol. 139. Proceedings of Machine Learning Research. PMLR, 2021, pp. 11920–11931. DOI: 10.48550/arXiv.2102.11271.

12. Lorenzo Canese et al. "Multi-agent reinforcement learning: A review of challenges and applications". In: *Applied Sciences* 11.11 (2021), p. 4948. DOI: 10.3390/app11114948.

13. Shangding Gu et al. "A Review of Safe Reinforcement Learning: Methods, Theories, and Applications". In: *IEEE Transactions on Pattern Analysis and Machine Intelligence* 46.12 (2024), pp. 11216–11235. DOI: 10.1109/TPAMI.2024.3457538.

14. Mridul Agarwal et al. "Reinforcement Learning for Mean-Field Game". In: *Algorithms* 15.3 (2022). ISSN: 1999-4893. DOI: 10.3390/a15030073.

15. Guibin Zhang et al. *The Landscape of Agentic Reinforcement Learning for LLMs: A Survey.* 2026. DOI: 10.48550/arXiv.2509.02547. arXiv: 2509.02547 [cs.AI].

16. Purna Chandra Rao Chinta and Laxmana Murthy Karaka. "Agentic AI and reinforcement learning: Towards more autonomous and adaptive ai systems". In: *Journal for Educators, Teachers and Trainers* https://jett.labosfor.com/index.php/jett/article/view/2699 (2020). DOI: 10.47750/jett.2020.11.01.20.

17. Hadi Nekoei et al. "Dealing With Non-stationarity in Decentralized Cooperative Multi-Agent Deep Reinforcement Learning via Multi-Timescale Learning". In: *Proceedings of The 2nd Conference on Lifelong Learning Agents*. Ed. by Sarath Chandar et al. Vol. 232. Proceedings of Machine Learning Research. PMLR, 2023, pp. 376–398. DOI: 10.48550/arXiv.2302.02792.

18. Patrick Butlin. "Reinforcement learning and artificial agency". In: *Mind"& Language* 39.1 (2024), pp. 22–38. DOI: https://doi.org/10.1111/mila.12458.

19. Ruichen Zhang et al. *Toward Agentic AI: Generative Information Retrieval Inspired Intelligent Communications and Networking*. 2025. DOI: 10.48550/arXiv.2502.16866. arXiv: 2502.16866 [cs.NI].

20. Ashis Kumar Pati. "Agentic AI: A Comprehensive Survey of Technologies, Applications, and Societal Implications". In: *IEEE Access* 13 (2025), pp. 151824–151837. DOI: 10.1109/ACCESS.2025.3585609.

21. Saptarshi Nath et al. *Policy Search, Retrieval, and Composition via Task Similarity in Collaborative Agentic Systems*. 2025. DOI: 10.48550/arXiv.2506.05577. arXiv: 2506.05577 [cs.LG].

22. Minhua Lin et al. *A Comprehensive Survey on Reinforcement Learning-based Agentic Search: Foundations, Roles, Optimizations, Evaluations, and Applications*. 2025. DOI: 10.48550/arXiv.2510.16724. arXiv: 2510.16724 [cs.AI]. URL: https://arxiv.org/abs/2510.16724.

23. Jongsoo Lee, Jonghyeok Park, and Soohee Han. "Overcoming Delayed Feedback in Reinforcement Learning Using Actor Ensembles". In: *International Journal of Control, Automation and Systems* 22.11 (2024), pp. 3266–3274. DOI: 10.1007/s12555-024-0043-9.

24. Ibrahim H. Ahmed et al. "Deep reinforcement learning for multi-agent interaction". In: *AI Communications* 35.4 (2022), pp. 357–368. DOI: 10.3233/AIC-220116.

25. Zexi Liu et al. *ML-Agent: Reinforcing LLM Agents for Autonomous Machine Learning Engineering*. 2025. DOI: 10.48550/arXiv.2505.23723. arXiv: 2505.23723 [cs.CL].

26. Afshin Oroojlooy and Davood Hajinezhad. "A review of cooperative multi-agent deep reinforcement learning". In: *Applied Intelligence* 53.11 (2023), pp. 13677–13722. DOI: 10.1007/s10489-022-04105-y.

27. Pedro F. Silvestre and Peter Pietzuch. "Systems Opportunities for LLM Fine-Tuning using Reinforcement Learning". In: *Proceedings of the 5th Workshop on Machine Learning and Systems*. EuroMLSys '25. World Trade Center, Rotterdam, Netherlands: Association for Computing Machinery, 2025, pp. 90–99. ISBN: 9798400715389. DOI: 10.1145/3721146.3721944.

28. Yuji Cao et al. "Survey on Large Language Model-Enhanced Reinforcement Learning: Concept, Taxonomy, and Methods". In: *IEEE Transactions on Neural Networks and Learning Systems* 36.6 (2025), pp. 9737–9757. DOI: 10.1109/TNNLS.2024.3497992.

29. Yue Wang and Shaofeng Zou. "Policy Gradient Method For Robust Reinforcement Learning". In: *Proceedings of the 39th International Conference on Machine Learning*. Ed. by Kamalika Chaudhuri et al. Vol. 162. Proceedings of Machine Learning Research. PMLR, 2022, pp. 23484–23526. DOI: 10.48550/arXiv.2205.07344.

30. Xu Wang et al. "Deep Reinforcement Learning: A Survey". In: *IEEE Transactions on Neural Networks and Learning Systems* 35.4 (2024), pp. 5064–5078. DOI: 10.1109/TNNLS.2022.3207346.

31. Saksham Sahai Srivastava and Vaneet Aggarwal. *A Technical Survey of Reinforcement Learning Techniques for Large Language Models*. 2025. DOI: 10.48550/arXiv.2507.04136. arXiv: 2507.04136 [cs.AI].

32. Kaiyan Zhang et al. *A Survey of Reinforcement Learning for Large Reasoning Models*. 2025. DOI: 10.48550/arXiv.2509.08827. arXiv: 2509.08827 [cs.CL].

33. Marc Rothmann and Mario Porrmann. "A Survey of Domain-Specific Architectures for Reinforcement Learning". In: *IEEE Access* 10 (2022), pp. 13753–13767. DOI: 10.1109/ACCESS.2022.3146518.

34. Amirfarhad Farhadi et al. "Domain adaptation in reinforcement learning: a comprehensive and systematic study". In: *Frontiers of Information Technology "& Electronic Engineering* 25.11 (2024), pp. 1446–1465. DOI: 10.1631/FITEE.2300668.

35. Ranjan Sapkota, Konstantinos I. Roumeliotis, and Manoj Karkee. "AI Agents vs. Agentic AI: A Conceptual taxonomy, applications and challenges". In: *Information Fusion* 126 (Feb. 2026), p. 103599. ISSN: 1566-2535. DOI: 10.1016/j.inffus.2025.103599. URL: http://dx.doi.org/10.1016/j.inffus.2025.103599.

36. Lang Mei et al. *AI-SearchPlanner: Modular Agentic Search via Pareto-Optimal Multi-Objective Reinforcement Learning*. 2025. DOI: 10.48550/arXiv.2508.20368. arXiv: 2508.20368 [cs.AI].

37. Jingda Wu et al. "Toward Human-in-the-Loop AI: Enhancing Deep Reinforcement Learning via Real-Time Human Guidance for Autonomous Driving". In: *Engineering* 21 (2023), pp. 75–91. ISSN: 2095-8099. DOI: https://doi.org/10.1016/j.eng.2022.05.017.

# Chapter 6
# Practical Application of the Case Study

**Abstract** This chapter presents a consolidated case study that demonstrates the practical instantiation of Agentic Artificial Intelligence (AI) in a real-world environmental monitoring context. Building on the conceptual, theoretical, and architectural foundations established in previous chapters, the chapter describes the design and operation of an agentic system deployed to support long-term analysis and decision-making in a complex natural environment. The case study illustrates how agent roles, coordination mechanisms, and learning dynamics are integrated within a unified system architecture. Particular attention is given to how reinforcement learning enables adaptive behaviour and how language-based interpretability supports transparency and human interaction. By examining system behaviour, adaptation processes, and observed outcomes, the chapter provides concrete insights into the practical challenges and benefits of deploying agentic systems in dynamic, real-world settings. The discussion highlights how Agentic AI enables persistent autonomy, collaborative reasoning, and meaningful human oversight, offering a tangible reference point for evaluating the applicability of agentic approaches beyond theoretical constructs.

## 6.1 Introducing the Case Study

The theoretical discussion surrounding Agentic architectures gains consistency and relevance when applied to concrete problems, especially those that require integrating multiple cognitive, social, and environmental dimensions. Among these challenges, water quality monitoring and management constitute a particularly fertile domain for exploring the potential of Agentic AI [1]. The case study presented here stems precisely from this framework: a system of intelligent agents designed to assess and classify lake pollution levels in the Azores using satellite imagery, combining Reinforcement Learning (RL), semantic analysis via Large Language Models (LLMs), and multi-agent coordination [2].

The choice of this context is not arbitrary. Azorean lakes are fragile ecosystems, sensitive to chemical and biological variations driven by both natural processes and human activities. Diffuse pollution, from agriculture, urban runoff, or atmospheric deposition, alters water composition, affecting biodiversity and ecological balance.

Traditionally, monitoring these lakes has relied on point-by-point measurements and physical models that, while rigorous, are incapable of capturing the system's dynamic complexity. The temporal and spatial variability of pollution sources requires adaptive, integrated approaches that combine remote data with contextual inference. It is precisely in this space of uncertainty and interdependence that Agentic AI demonstrates its relevance [3].

The proposed system is conceptually organised around a community of specialised agents, each responsible for a distinct dimension of ecological tasks. There are agents dedicated to perception, tasking to extract and interpret visual information from satellite imagery, decision agents that learn classification policies based on environmental feedback, and coordination agents that ensure coherence between local interpretations and the global ecological framework. The latter uses LLMs to interpret textual descriptions of environmental parameters, scientific reports, and historical patterns, and to translate them into semantic representations usable by other agents. In this way, the LLM acts as a cognitive mediator, allowing the network of agents to transform numerical and linguistic data into operational knowledge.

The system is therefore composed of several Agentic AI agents, whose combined goal is to generate a textual representation of the Water Quality assessment. However, learning is not purely individual for that particular agent. Therefore, it is then verified by another agent powered by a more capable reasoning LLM. Thus, each agent's objective must consider not only its performance but also its coherence with the collective. This principle approximates the system as a multi-agent cooperative learning model, in which knowledge is shared, and rewards are partially shared. This sharing creates a cognitive synergy effect: the greater the harmony between agents, the more accurate and stable the global classification becomes.

The participation of each agent in the conversation, performing different tasks, is ensured through a group chat that facilitates communication among them [4]. Some agents have specific tasks and objectives for data collection and preprocessing to ensure newly available data aligns with what other agents expect. After the preprocessing, an agent is responsible for classifying water quality. Another one is the decision-support textual representation, where the classification is represented in human language to enable understanding of the outcome, such as inferring possible causes (e.g., increased precipitation or agricultural runoff) and articulating these hypotheses [5]. A critical analysis is needed to evaluate the previous textual representation to ensure it is coherent and respects ethical and biological guidelines. Finally, RL assures that the agents adapt to the previously mentioned guidelines.

Unlike traditional pollution detection systems, which rely on fixed thresholds or purely supervised algorithms, the Agentic system outlined here is reflexive and dialogical [6]. The interaction between agents promotes a continuous process of mutual verification, in which interpretations are tested, adjusted, and justified linguistically. Each analysis cycle is accompanied by a symbolic discussion, a kind of internal deliberation, mediated by the LLM. This mechanism approximates a rudimentary form of collective reasoning, in which knowledge emerges from interaction without direct human intervention [7]. Thus, decision-making about the ecological state of the lakes does not result from an isolated calculation, but from a distributed deliberation.

From a scientific perspective, this case study allows us to explore central questions about communication between heterogeneous agents. Satellite imagery produces high-dimensional numerical data, while ecological descriptions are textual and qualitative [8]. The integration of these two domains requires a common language, which LLMs provide through shared semantic representations. Natural Language Processing (NLP) thus becomes an instrument of cognitive interoperability, replacing the old paradigm of algorithmic coding with an interpretive model. This fusion of the visual, numerical, and linguistic is one of the most original contributions of Agentic architecture: it transforms environmental analysis into an interdisciplinary reasoning process, in which the boundaries between perception and interpretation are blurred [9].

Beyond the technical dimension, the case of the Azores lakes introduces an ethical and epistemological reflection on the role of AI in environmental sustainability. An Agentic system that decides on water quality is not neutral: it influences public policies, mitigation strategies, and social perceptions. Its autonomy, therefore, requires mechanisms of ethical alignment that ensure decisions respect ecological and social values. In the case under analysis, alignment is ensured by a normative layer embedded in the supervising agent, which can weigh the consequences of each decision on the ecosystem's balance. This process does not replace human judgment, but instead creates a new form of cognitive collaboration, in which humans and artificial agents share epistemological and ethical responsibility for environmental protection [10].

The practical implementation of this system, albeit in its experimental phase, demonstrates how Agentic AI can transform the way we understand and manage complex natural phenomena [11]. The lakes cease to be passive monitoring objects and become a shared cognitive environment in which agents learn, communicate, and interpret in real time. The Azores case thus reveals the potential of an emerging computational ecology, in which AI not only observes the world but also actively participates in its preservation. This model represents a significant step toward an Agentic environmental science, in which Machine Learning (ML), symbolic reasoning, and social interaction come together in an architecture guided by ecological responsibility.

The importance of this case study transcends the technical domain of environmental monitoring. It exemplifies the convergence between theory and practice in Agentic AI: it demonstrates that autonomy, communication, and cooperative learning are not abstract concepts, but operational dimensions that can be materialised in concrete systems. In doing so, it also reveals a new relationship between technology and nature, a relationship based on cognitive co-evolution, in which AI becomes an epistemological ally of sustainability. In the context of this book, the Azores lakes are more than an experimental setting: it is a microcosm of the Agentic paradigm, a space where the transition from AI as a tool to AI as a cognitive partner of the Earth can be observed [12].

Given the problem domain's characteristics and requirements, an Agentic AI architecture was designed to support long-term autonomy, adaptive decision-making, and collaborative reasoning. The next section presents an overview of this system, highlighting its main components and their interactions.

## 6.2  Conceptual Mapping of Agentic Principles

The case study presented in this work operationalises the theoretical foundations of Agentic AI through a concrete, end-to-end MAS designed for water quality classification and explanation. Rather than treating Agentic AI as an abstract or purely conceptual paradigm, the framework embodies its core principles by translating them into explicit architectural, behavioural, and learning-oriented design choices. This section establishes a conceptual bridge between the theoretical constructs discussed earlier and their practical realisation, demonstrating how agentic principles can be systematically instantiated within a real-world intelligent system.

A central principle of Agentic AI is autonomy realised through functional decomposition. In the case study, autonomy is achieved by structuring the system as a collection of specialised agents, each responsible for a distinct cognitive or operational role. Data acquisition, preprocessing, prediction, explanation, evaluation, and reinforcement are not implemented as sequential stages within a monolithic pipeline, but as independent agents operating according to local objectives and partial information. This design directly reflects classical Multi-Agent Systems (MAS) theory, where intelligence is distributed rather than centralised, while simultaneously extending it through agentic notions of persistent goals, self-directed behaviour, and adaptive decision-making. Each agent maintains its own operational logic and learning dynamics, enabling the system to function as a collection of semi-independent decision-makers rather than a rigid workflow.

Inter-agent coordination within the framework is realised through structured message passing, which serves as the primary mechanism for communication and information exchange. Agents communicate observations, intermediate outputs, evaluations, and feedback without exposing internal state or requiring global synchronisation. This mirrors decentralised coordination models in MAS theory, in which cooperation emerges from interaction rather than from explicit orchestration. From an agentic perspective, this communication is not merely procedural but semantic: messages carry meaning related to system goals, performance, and quality. This allows coordination to remain flexible and adaptive, supporting extensibility and robustness as agents can be modified, replaced, or augmented without destabilising the overall system.

Learning and adaptation constitute another critical dimension of the conceptual mapping. In the proposed system, learning is not confined to a single optimisation phase or component, but is distributed across multiple agents and across time. RL is employed to optimise the performance of Deep Learning (DL) classifiers, while a separate reinforcement-driven process governs the quality of explanations generated by language-based agents. This separation reflects an agentic view of intelligence as multi-level and modular, where distinct agents optimise different behavioural dimensions while contributing to a shared system-level objective. Importantly, learning is embedded within continuous operational loops, aligning with the agentic principle that intelligence emerges through sustained interaction rather than static training.

NLP plays a unifying and structuring role within the system, functioning as more than a user-facing interface. Explanations, evaluations, critiques, and corrective feedback are all mediated through language, enabling agents to operate within a shared semantic space. This design choice directly maps theoretical advances in language-enabled agentic systems to practical implementation. Language serves as a cognitive substrate through which agents reason about model behaviour, articulate uncertainty, assess the quality of explanations, and guide reinforcement processes. By grounding interaction in NLP, the system aligns machine reasoning with human interpretability, reinforcing transparency and facilitating meaningful human-in-the-loop engagement.

The framework also embodies the agentic principle of reflection and self-assessment. Generated explanations are not treated as terminal outputs, but as intermediate artefacts subject to evaluation, critique, and refinement. Dedicated evaluative agents assess explanation quality according to predefined criteria and generate structured feedback that informs subsequent learning. This explicit modelling of critique and revision mirrors theoretical notions of reflective agents capable of monitoring their own behaviour and improving over time. Reflection is therefore not an implicit by-product of optimisation but an explicit architectural component of the system.

At the system level, intelligence emerges from the interaction of agents rather than from any single component. No individual agent possesses complete knowledge of the task, the environment, or the system's global state. Instead, meaningful predictions and explanations arise through cooperative execution, iterative feedback, and mutual constraint. This emergent behaviour directly reflects foundational ideas in MAS theory while extending them through agentic mechanisms such as language-based coordination, reinforcement-guided self-improvement, and long-term operational coherence. The system's capabilities are thus greater than the sum of its parts, illustrating how agentic intelligence arises from structured interaction rather than isolated computation.

Crucially, the case study also reflects the agentic emphasis on temporal continuity and process-oriented intelligence. The system is designed to operate across extended time horizons, where predictions, explanations, evaluations, and learning cycles inform one another continuously. Rather than optimising for a single output, the framework maintains coherence across repeated interactions, allowing both predictive performance and explanatory quality to evolve. This mapping highlights a fundamental shift from task-bound AI systems toward agentic systems that manage processes, objectives, and quality over time.

In summary, the case study demonstrates how the theoretical principles of Agentic AI, such as autonomy, decentralisation, communication, learning, reflection, emergence, and semantic coordination, can be systematically mapped onto a practical implementation. The framework does not merely apply agent-based techniques, but realises an integrated agentic system in which prediction, explanation, evaluation, and improvement are tightly interconnected. This conceptual mapping confirms that Agentic AI provides a coherent and actionable foundation for building intelligent systems capable of sustained autonomy, adaptive learning, and meaningful interaction within complex real-world domains.

## 6.3   Architectural Implementation

The practical application realises the proposed Agentic AI framework through a concrete multi-agent architecture implemented using AutoGen. The system is designed as a cooperative ensemble of specialised agents that collectively perform data processing, prediction, explanation, evaluation, and continuous improvement. Rather than implementing these functionalities as a linear pipeline, the architecture instantiates each capability as an autonomous yet communicative agent, aligned with the agentic principles discussed earlier in this work.

The overall architecture can be conceptually divided into five interacting layers: data acquisition, data preparation, prediction, explanation and evaluation, and reinforcement-driven adaptation. This aligns with the Cross-Industry Standard Process for Data Mining (CRISP-DM) methodology [13]. It defines the digital science lifecycle, particularly in data handling, comprising 6 phases: Business Understanding, Data Understanding, Data Preparation, Modelling, Evaluation, and Deployment, as shown in Fig. 6.1. These can be directly aligned with the tasks of each agent: an agent will retrieve the data, another will prepare it, then a DL model will be applied, and subsequently an explanation will be created, evaluated, and used to reinforce the explanations generated.

At the foundation of the architecture are agents responsible for data acquisition and preparation. These agents handle the retrieval of satellite imagery and in-situ data, as well as the preprocessing steps necessary to prepare the data for inference. By isolating data-related responsibilities within dedicated agents, the system ensures that changes in data sources, preprocessing strategies, or temporal configurations can be incorporated without affecting downstream reasoning or explanation mechanisms. This separation of concerns reinforces modularity and supports scalability across different geographical locations and temporal resolutions.

The data acquisition layer is handled by the Image Collector Agent, which serves as the system's interface to external data sources. This agent is responsible for retriev-

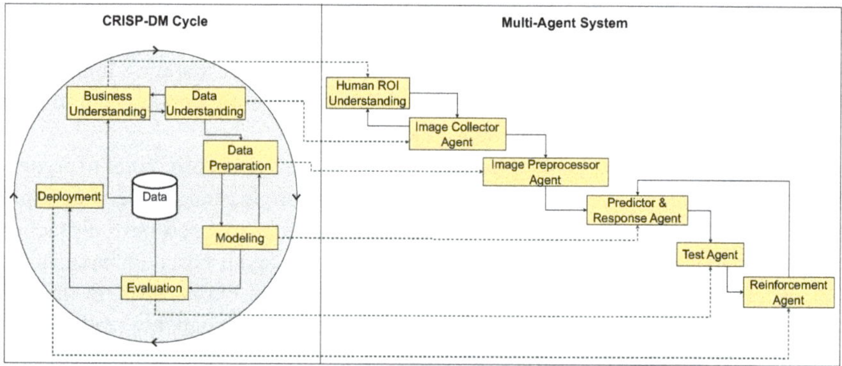


**Fig. 6.1**  Practical application architecture

ing satellite imagery based on user-specified temporal and spatial inputs. By isolating data retrieval within a dedicated agent, the system ensures that changes in data availability, satellite products, or geographical scope do not propagate unnecessary complexity to other components.

All agents within the proposed architecture adhere to a common structural and execution pattern defined by AutoGen's agent abstractions, enabling substantial consolidation of implementation and documentation. Each agent inherits from either *BaseChatAgent*, used for deterministic or procedural tasks, or *AssistantAgent*, employed when interaction with a language model is required. An example of such implementation can be observed in Listing 6.1.

```python
from autogen_agentchat.agents import BaseChatAgent

class ImageCollectorAgent(BaseChatAgent):
    def __init__(self, name, system_message):
        super().__init__(name=name, description=system_message)
```

**Listing 6.1**  Image Collector Initialisation

For the agent to properly receive the message, an *on_messages* method needs to be created, with the messages passed as a parameter, as shown in Listing 6.2. We collect the last message from the *messages* parameter and save it to *last_message*, making it easier to use. A wrapper called $try - except$ is then used, ensuring proper handling when an exception is thrown. Inside the $try$ clause, the $json$ is loaded from the $last_message$, and the $date, location$, and $size$ are saved to separate variables, so the Agent knows when and where to retrieve the data. In the $exception$ clause, either a $TypeError$ or $KeyError$ is caught and handled by returning an error message.

In all cases, agents expose an identical lifecycle: initialisation via a constructor that forwards the agent's name and role-defining system message to the superclass, message handling through an *on_messages* method that extracts and parses the most recent GroupChat message.

```python
def on_messages(self, messages):
    last_message = messages[-1]["content"]

    try:
        last_message = json.loads(last_message)
        date = last_message.get("date")
        location = last_message.get("location")
        size = last_message.get("size")
    except (TypeError, KeyError):
        return "Invalid input format. Please provide 'date' and '
    location'."
```

**Listing 6.2**  Image Collector Message Treatment

Once the message has been properly handled, the next step is to retrieve the data. Consequently, Listing 6.3 has a save location named *images_folder*, which is created with its corresponding path, and if it already exists, all data within it is deleted, and it is ensured to exist. Then a $try - except$ block is created again, where, inside the $try$ clause, the remote call to the corresponding site is made, passing the necessary parameters. In the $except$ clause, an error message is returned that states the exception it caught.

```python
images_folder = "./images"
if os.path.exists(images_folder):
    shutil.rmtree(images_folder)
os.makedirs(images_folder, exist_ok=True)

try:
    images_path = self.fetch_copernicus_images(date=date,
location=location, size=size)
except Exception as e:
    return f"Error fetching images: {e}"
```

**Listing 6.3**  Image Collector Data Retrieval

Once data retrieval is completed, the Image Collector Agent prepares a forward message using a structured return statement, as shown in Listing 6.4. The agent encapsulates its output in a JSON-formatted payload that includes the image path, acquisition date, and location metadata, all of which are required by downstream agents for subsequent processing. This return-based message propagation mechanism is common across the entire multi-agent architecture. Although the semantic content of the forwarded payload varies between agents, ranging from satellite image references and preprocessed tensors to predicted classes, explanation texts, evaluation scores, and reinforcement signals, the surrounding control logic remains invariant. Each agent serialises its task-specific outputs into a structured $json$ response and returns it to the GroupChat, ensuring a uniform communication protocol throughout the system. For conciseness, this pattern is illustrated only once here; equivalent forward-message constructions are employed by all other agents in the pipeline.

```python
return {
    "content": json.dumps({
        "images_path": images_path,
        "date": date,
        "location": location
    })
}
```

**Listing 6.4**  Image Collector Forward Message

Listing 6.5 shows how to set up the Agent in the AutoGen environment. First, we need to create a variable to store the agent, then instantiate it using an import called $ImageCollectorAgent$, which we developed above. The constructor accepts the $name$ and $system\_message$, where the first provides the agent with a name and the second specifies the task the agent will complete.

```
from Agents.ImageCollectorAgent import ImageCollectorAgent

collector_agent = ImageCollectorAgent(
    name="ImageCollectorAgent",
    system_message="Fetches Sentinel-2 images based on date and
    location input.",
)
```

**Listing 6.5** Image Collector Agent Setup

Once data is retrieved, responsibility is transferred to the Image Pre-processor Agent, which performs all preparation steps required for downstream analysis. This includes filtering cloud-contaminated images, mosaicking usable imagery when necessary, and generating domain-specific indices relevant to water quality assessment. By encapsulating preprocessing logic within a single agent, the framework maintains a clear separation between raw data handling and predictive reasoning, thereby reinforcing modularity and reproducibility. As before, an agent for this specific and linear task is developed using the same principles as the Image Collector Agent.

The agent's task needs to be developed, as it is specific and requires distinct preparation methods. Listing 6.6 lists the methods needed to perform these operations. It starts by using *untar_daily_structure* to extract the images, passing the data path as a parameter. It is followed by *average_months*, which calculates cloud coverage using the *cloud_threshold* to determine whether to average. Next up, *applyIndexes* ensures that different indices are applied to the satellite images, providing much more information about specific parameters of the observed scenario. The entry *save_rgb_image* ensures that a True Colour image exists, and to finish it off, *clean_all_months* cleans the directory of unused data.

```
    untar_daily_structure(images_path)
    average_months(cloud_threshold=80.0, output_dir=images_path)
    applyIndexes(images_path)
    save_rgb_image(images_path)
    images_path = clean_all_months(images_path)
```

**Listing 6.6** Image Collector Data Retrieval

The agent's task stops by preparing a message to be returned, saving the *output_dir*, the path to the data, and the *location* of the observed scenario as *json*.

Finally, when initialising the agent in the AutoGen environment, it creates a variable called *preprocessor_agent* to store the Agent, as shown in Listing 6.7. It uses the *ImagePreProcessorAgent* created earlier, together with the *system_message* for its specific task.

```
1  from Agents.ImagePreProcessorAgent import ImagePreProcessorAgent
2
3  preprocessor_agent = ImagePreProcessorAgent(
4      name="ImagePreProcessorAgent",
5      system_message="Preprocesses the satellite image bands for
         model prediction.",
6  )
```

**Listing 6.7**  Image Pre-Processor Agent Setup

The predictive component of the system is encapsulated in a dedicated Predictor Agent, which loads and executes DL models for water quality classification. These models are not static artefacts; they are produced through an upstream RLâŁ"driven optimisation process in which hyperparameters are iteratively adjusted to maximise classification performance. While the optimisation logic is conceptually and operationally distinct, the Predictor Agent operates autonomously at inference time, reflecting an agentic architecture in which performance optimisation and decision execution are treated as complementary but separate cognitive functions.

Beyond conventional inference, the Predictor Agent functions as an active element within a broader adaptive learning ecosystem. Its predictions directly inform downstream explanatory agents and contribute to the system's overall interpretability, while feedback from evaluative components influences future optimisation cycles. This bidirectional interaction elevates prediction from a terminal processing step to a dynamic participant in an evolving, self-improving agentic system for water quality assessment.

The usual initialisation of the agent to perform its classifications using previously collected and processed data. Following up, Listing 6.8 highlights how the agent performs its task: it needs to load the specialised DL models using *model_path*. Then, the model is loaded using the *load_model* method, with the previously mentioned path to the models and the site's *location*. When the model is loaded, it will perform classification on the data from *images_path* using *model* and also provide *location*. The classification is then converted to a string using the method *prediction_to_string*. At the end, the agent needs to count down *steps_remaining* to keep track.

```
1      model_path = './TrainedModels'
2      model = self.load_model(model_path, location)
3      classification = self.predict(model, images_path, location)
4      classification = self.prediction_to_string(classification)
5      steps_remaining = steps_remaining - 1
```

**Listing 6.8**  Predictor Classification

Lastly, the agent needs to create a final message to be passed on, which includes the *classification* out of the *possible_classifications*, the *location*, the path to the *truecolour_image*, the updated *steps_remaining* and its *status*.

For agent creation in the AutoGen environment, the *Predictor Agent* is imported and used to instantiate it by passing the *name* and the *system_message* that describes its task.

```python
from Agents.PredictorAgent import PredictorAgent

predictor_agent = PredictorAgent(
    name="PredictorAgent",
    system_message="Loads a trained model for the specified
    location and predicts water quality.",
)
```

**Listing 6.9**  Predictor Agent Setup

Once a water quality classification is generated, responsibility shifts to the Response Agent, which transforms numerical model outputs into natural-language explanations. Rather than relying on templated or rule-based descriptions, this agent leverages a large language model to generate contextualised, human-readable narratives that describe the meaning, implications, and potential causes of the predicted water quality state. These explanations incorporate relevant environmental variables, temporal patterns, and aspects of the model's learned behaviour, enabling users to understand not only what was predicted, but why.

Crucially, explanation is treated as a first-class artefact within the system rather than as a post-hoc addition. By embedding explanation generation directly into the agentic pipeline, the architecture elevates interpretability from an auxiliary feature to a core system capability. The Response Agent thus serves as the primary interface between the system's internal reasoning processes and human understanding, aligning the overall design with broader objectives of transparency, trustworthiness, and responsible deployment of applied AI.

Before generating explanations, the Response Agent must be defined with a clear and static responsibility: transforming model predictions into natural-language explanations. Since this task involves interaction with a language model rather than deterministic data processing, the agent is implemented using the *Assistant Agent* class provided by AutoGen, which is specifically designed for LLM-driven behaviour. Listing 6.10 shows the initialisation of the Response Agent; it will be the same for the Test Agent and the Reinforcement Agent.

```python
from autogen import AssistantAgent

class ResponseAgent(AssistantAgent):
    def __init__(self, name, system_message, llm_config=None):
        super().__init__(name=name, description=system_message,
        llm_config=llm_config, max_consecutive_auto_reply=1001)
```

**Listing 6.10**  Response Agent Initialisation

The agent class inherits directly from *Assistant Agent*, reusing its core conversational capabilities while allowing custom logic to be layered on top. As with previous agents, an *init* method is defined to pass configuration parameters during instantiation. These include the agent's name, a *system_message* that constrains its role, and an optional *llm_config* specifying the language model to be used.

The call to *super* ensures that the parent class is correctly initialised, while the *max_consecutive_auto_reply* parameter allows the agent to generate extended responses when necessary.

After the message has been successfully parsed, the agent generates a natural-language response. Listing 6.11 illustrates the reply generation step. Rather than constructing explanations using predefined rules or templates, the agent delegates this task to a language model via the *generate_reply* method. The prompt passed to the model includes the prediction and its context, enabling it to produce a coherent, human-readable explanation tailored to the specific scenario.

```
response = self.generate_reply(messages=[{"role": "user", "
    content": prompt}])
```

**Listing 6.11**  Response Agent Reply Generation

Finally, once an explanation has been generated, the agent prepares a structured response to be forwarded downstream. The return message is formatted as JSON and includes the original prompt, the generated explanation, the path to the true-colour image, the predicted class, and the remaining step count. A status flag is also included to signal successful completion of the agent's task.

Listing 6.12 demonstrates how the Response Agent is instantiated within the Auto-Gen environment. A variable is created to store the agent instance, and the previously defined ResponseAgent class is initialised with a descriptive system message that explicitly constrains its role to explanation generation rather than prediction. The *llm_config* parameter specifies the language model used, allowing the explanation layer to be tuned independently of the predictive components.

```
from Agents.ResponseAgent import ResponseAgent

response_agent = ResponseAgent(
    name="ResponseAgent",
    system_message="Explains the water quality prediction, there
    is no need to try to predict, the prediction is already
    provided.",
    llm_config=llm_config_small
)
```

**Listing 6.12**  Response Agent Setup

To ensure explanation quality and alignment, the architecture introduces a dedicated Test Agent that evaluates generated explanations using a more capable language model acting as an independent judge. This agent critiques explanations across multiple dimensions, including coherence, relevance, clarity for non-expert users, and faithfulness to the underlying prediction. In addition to assigning quantitative quality scores, the Test Agent produces alternative responses that exemplify both stronger and weaker explanations, providing concrete reference points for evaluation.

Essentially, these assessments are not merely diagnostic. The feedback generated by the Test Agent is treated as a structured learning signal and is routed back into the system's optimisation process. A reinforcement-driven agent leverages this feedback to iteratively refine explanation strategies, closing the loop between generation, evaluation, and improvement. This reflective cycle operationalises theoretical notions of self-monitoring and adaptive behaviour, embedding continuous improvement of explanation quality directly into the agentic architecture rather than treating it as an external validation step.

Once the Response Agent has produced an explanation, the Test Agent initiates an evaluation phase. As shown in Listing 6.13, the agent uses the *generate_reply* method twice, each time with a distinct prompt. The first prompt (*score_prompt*) instructs the language model to critique the explanation and assign a quality score, typically along dimensions such as coherence, relevance, clarity, and faithfulness to the underlying prediction. This step yields a structured evaluation that can be interpreted as a reward signal.

```
test_response = self.generate_reply(messages=[{"role": "user", "content": score_prompt}])

counterpart_response = self.generate_reply(messages=[{"role": "user", "content": counterpart_prompt}])
```

**Listing 6.13** Test Agent Evaluation & Counterpart Response

In addition to scoring, the Test Agent generates a counterpart response using a second prompt (*counterpart_prompt*). This counterpart represents an alternative explanation, intentionally framed as either a stronger or weaker version of the original. By producing such contrasts, the Test Agent provides concrete reference examples that help operationalise abstract quality judgments. These paired explanations are particularly useful for reinforcement-driven learning, as they clarify what constitutes improvement or degradation in explanation quality.

Following evaluation, the Test Agent records all relevant artefacts for traceability and downstream learning. Listing 6.14 shows how the agent logs the original prompt, the generated explanation, the computed reward, the rationale for the evaluation, the counterpart response, and the associated true-colour image path. This logging mechanism ensures that explanation generation and evaluation are fully auditable and reproducible, enabling both offline analysis and iterative refinement of the system.

```
self.log_sample(original_prompt, explanation, reward, reason, counterpart_response, truecolor_path)
```

**Listing 6.14** Test Agent Log

Listing 6.15 illustrates how the Test Agent is instantiated within the AutoGen environment. A dedicated variable, *test_agent*, is created to store the agent instance, ensuring it can be referenced and integrated into the multi-agent workflow by importing the agent developed before.

The agent is initialised using the custom TestAgent class, which encapsulates all evaluation and logging functionality described previously. The name parameter uniquely identifies the agent within the system, while the *system_message* explicitly defines its role as an evaluator of natural-language explanations rather than a generative or predictive component. This constraint ensures that the agent consistently adopts a critical and analytical stance when interacting with explanation outputs.

The *llm_config* parameter specifies a more capable language model, reflecting the increased reasoning demands associated with explanation evaluation and quality assessment. Finally, the *log_path* argument defines the location where evaluation samples are persistently stored in *jsonl* format. This log serves as a structured memory of explanations, scores, and counterpart responses, enabling reproducibility, offline analysis, and reinforcement-driven optimisation.

```python
from Agents.TestAgent import TestAgent

test_agent = TestAgent(
    name="TestAgent",
    system_message="Evaluates the quality of natural language
    explanations and logs the sample.",
    llm_config=llm_config_big,
    log_path='./Logs/reinforcement_data.jsonl'
)
```

**Listing 6.15**  Test Agent Setup

The reinforcement layer is governed by the Reinforcement Agent, which closes the system's adaptive loop. This agent aggregates evaluation outcomes and selectively uses high-quality examples to fine-tune the explanatory language model through RL. Rather than relying on external supervision or static datasets, the system improves itself by learning from its own successes and failures. This creates a self-improving cycle in which prediction, explanation, evaluation, and learning are tightly interconnected.

Erstwhile evaluation data has been accumulated by the Test Agent; responsibility shifts to the Reinforcement Agent, whose role is to refine explanation-generation behaviour using RL. Listing 6.16 shows the invocation of the RL procedure that operates over the logged evaluation data produced during prior interaction cycles.

```python
GRPO_RL(model_name="unsloth/gemma-3-1b-it", dataset_path="./Logs/
    reinforcement_data.jsonl", dataset_type="json",
    max_seq_length=1024, max_prompt_length=256, quantization_type
    ="Q8_0", output_dir_LoRA="gemma3", output_dir_finetune="
    gemma3-finetune")
```

**Listing 6.16**  Reinforcement Agent Task

The reinforcement process is implemented by the *GRPO_RL* routine, which optimises the policy of a pre-trained language model. The *model_name* parameter specifies the base model used for explanation generation, while the *dataset_path* points to the *jsonl* log file created by the Test Agent. This dataset contains structured samples consisting of prompts, generated explanations, evaluation rewards, and comparative counterparts, forming the foundation for reinforcement-driven learning. The *dataset_type* parameter explicitly defines the dataset format to ensure correct parsing.

Several configuration parameters control the training dynamics. The *max_seq_length* and *max_prompt_length* parameters constrain the model's input and output sizes, ensuring stable and efficient optimisation. The *quantization_type* argument enables low-precision training to reduce memory usage while preserving performance. Finally, two output directories are specified: one for storing the intermediate LoRA adapters (*output_dir_LoRA*) and another for saving the fully fine-tuned model (*output_dir_finetune*).

Listing 6.17 shows the initialisation of the Reinforcement Agent within the Auto-Gen environment. A dedicated variable, *reinforcement_agent*, is created to store the agent instance, enabling its integration into the broader multi-agent pipeline.

```python
from Agents.ReinforcementAgent import ReinforcementAgent

reinforcement_agent = ReinforcementAgent(
    name="ReinforcementAgent",
    system_message="Handles reinforcement learning tasks.",
    llm_config=llm_config_big,
    log_path='./Logs/reinforcement_data.jsonl'
)
```

**Listing 6.17**  Reinforcement Agent Setup

The agent is instantiated using the custom ReinforcementAgent class, which encapsulates all logic related to reinforcement-driven optimisation. The name parameter uniquely identifies the agent within the system, while the *system_message* explicitly defines its role as handling RL tasks rather than prediction or explanation. This clear role specification ensures conceptual separation between inference, evaluation, and optimisation.

The *llm_config* parameter specifies a more capable language model, reflecting the increased reasoning and planning requirements associated with RL workflows. The *log_path* argument points to the *jsonl* file containing evaluation samples produced by the Test Agent. This shared log serves as the interface between explanation evaluation and RL, enabling the agent to refine generation strategies based on accumulated feedback.

Coordination among all agents is achieved through AutoGen's GroupChat mechanism, which serves as the system's shared interaction space. Each agent publishes observations, intermediate outputs, and decisions to the GroupChat, ensuring that relevant context is visible across the architecture. The GroupChatManager functions as the orchestration layer, regulating turn-taking and determining which agent should act at each stage of execution. Rather than enforcing a rigid execution order, this conversational orchestration allows the system to adapt dynamically, enabling agents to respond to evolving system states and intermediate results.

Listing 6.18 shows the configuration of the GroupChat and its interaction constraints. The *allowed_speaker_transitions* dictionary explicitly defines which agent is permitted to act after another, encoding the logical progression of the pipeline. Following the prediction, control transitions to the Response Agent for explanation generation. The resulting explanation is then passed to the Test Agent for evaluation, after which the Reinforcement Agent processes the accumulated feedback. Finally, control returns to the Predictor Agent, closing the loop and enabling iterative system refinement.

The GroupChat is initialised with the participating agents, an empty message history, and a maximum number of interaction rounds. By specifying interaction constraints rather than a fixed execution sequence, the architecture supports adaptive behaviour while preserving correctness and stability. This conversational orchestration model aligns with the system's agentic design philosophy, allowing agents to operate autonomously within well-defined coordination boundaries and enabling continuous cycles of prediction, explanation, evaluation, and learning.

```
allowed_speaker_transitions = {
    predictor_agent: [response_agent, predictor_agent],
    response_agent: [test_agent],
    test_agent: [reinforcement_agent],
    reinforcement_agent: [predictor_agent],
}


group_chat = GroupChat(
    agents=[predictor_agent, response_agent, test_agent,
    reinforcement_agent],
    messages=[],
    max_round=1000,
    allowed_speaker_transitions=allowed_speaker_transitions,
)
```

**Listing 6.18**   AutoGen's GroupChat Setup

NLP plays a central architectural role throughout the implementation. Messages exchanged between agents encode not only task instructions but also reasoning, critiques, and justifications. This design choice allows heterogeneous agents, ranging from data-processing components to language-based evaluators, to operate within a shared semantic space. As a result, the architecture supports both machine-level coordination and human interpretability, enabling seamless inspection, debugging, and extension of system behaviour.

In general, the architectural implementation demonstrates how Agentic AI principles can be instantiated in a real-world application through deliberate design choices. Autonomy is realised through specialised agents, coordination through structured communication, learning through reinforcement-driven feedback loops, and interpretability through language-mediated interaction. By grounding these principles in an operational AutoGen-based architecture, the system moves beyond conceptual abstraction and illustrates how agentic design can support robust, adaptive, and explainable AI in complex applied domains such as water quality assessment.

The architecture of the proposed Agentic AI framework is designed to operationalise intelligent behaviour as a coordinated process among specialised agents rather than as a monolithic pipeline. Inspired by the CRISP-DM methodology, the system decomposes the overall problem of water quality classification and explanation into distinct cognitive and operational stages, each assigned to a dedicated agent. This design reflects the agentic principle that intelligence emerges from interaction, cooperation, and iterative refinement rather than from isolated computation.

At a high level, the architecture follows a sequential flow that begins with data acquisition and culminates in human-interpretable explanations. However, this sequence is not rigid. Instead, it is augmented by feedback loops that enable continuous improvement through RL. The system thus combines structured progression with adaptive behaviour, allowing agents to revisit earlier stages when improvement signals are detected.

Crucially, the system does not rely on a central controller that dictates execution order. Instead, coordination is achieved through AutoGen's GroupChat mechanism, where agents publish messages and observe shared context. The GroupChatManager regulates participation, ensuring orderly interaction while preserving decentralisation. This conversational orchestration allows agents to act autonomously while remaining aware of the system's global state.

From an architectural perspective, the framework exemplifies several defining characteristics of Agentic AI. Intelligence is distributed rather than centralised, learning is continuous rather than episodic, and communication is semantic rather than procedural. Each agent operates with local objectives and partial knowledge, yet the system as a whole exhibits coherent, goal-directed behaviour.

In summary, the architecture demonstrates how Agentic AI can be realised as a practical, end-to-end system that integrates perception, prediction, explanation, evaluation, and learning within a unified multi-agent framework. By grounding abstract agentic principles in concrete architectural decisions, the framework illustrates a scalable and interpretable approach to building intelligent systems capable of sustained autonomy and meaningful human interaction.

As learning continuously modifies agent behaviour and decision processes, maintaining transparency becomes essential for effective oversight and collaboration. The following section, therefore, addresses how interpretability is embedded within the agentic system, enabling agents to communicate their reasoning processes and support meaningful human interaction.

## 6.4  LLM-based Interpretability

The interpretability mechanisms are operationalised in this work through an LLM-driven agentic architecture that generates transparent, contextualised, and user-oriented explanations for water-quality predictions. Rather than treating interpretability as an auxiliary component applied after inference, the proposed system integrates explanation generation, evaluation, and refinement directly into the decision-making framework. This design reflects the view that interpretability is not a static artefact but a dynamic process that evolves alongside prediction and learning.

At the core of this application is the use of LLMs as interpretive agents that transform model outputs, intermediate reasoning signals, and domain context into NLP explanations. The predictive component of the system produces water quality classifications based on satellite imagery and associated features, using specialised DL models tailored to the Region of Interest. These predictions, while numerically meaningful, are not directly interpretable by non-technical users. To address this gap, the system employs a dedicated response-generating agent that receives structured outputs from the predictive model, including the predicted class, confidence indicators, and contextual metadata, and converts them into explanatory narratives tailored to the environmental domain.

This explanation process goes beyond simple verbalisation of predictions. The LLM-based agent contextualises results by relating them to known environmental standards, typical seasonal behaviour, and potential ecological implications. For example, a predicted decline in water quality is not merely reported as a class change but explained in terms of possible contributing factors and expected consequences. In doing so, the system aligns interpretability with domain reasoning rather than purely model-centric explanations.

A defining feature of the proposed application is that interpretability is embedded within an agentic interaction loop rather than delivered as a single output. Generated explanations are evaluated by an independent test agent that serves as a critical assessor rather than a passive observer. This agent analyses explanations for clarity, coherence, factual consistency, and alignment with the underlying prediction. By assigning scores and generating comparative examples of stronger or weaker explanations, the system introduces an explicit quality signal into the interpretability process.

These evaluation signals are then used to drive RL, enabling the system to improve its explanatory capabilities over time. High-quality explanations are reinforced, while weaker explanations are discouraged. This feedback-driven mechanism transforms interpretability from a static design choice into a learnable capability. As a result, the system does not merely explain its outputs; it learns to explain them more effectively through structured feedback.

Importantly, the agentic design ensures that explanations are grounded in observable system behaviour. Explanations are generated based on verifiable inputs, including model predictions, agent messages, and system state, rather than free-form speculation. This grounding mitigates the risk of explanation hallucination, a known limitation of LLM-based interpretability, by constraining explanation generation to information that is explicitly available within the system. In this sense, interpretability is anchored to operational transparency rather than narrative plausibility alone.

From a broader perspective, this application demonstrates how LLM-based interpretability can be effectively integrated into real-world AI systems through agentic design. Rather than relying on isolated explanation techniques, interpretability emerges from coordinated interactions among specialised agents, each contributing to transparency, evaluation, and learning. This approach aligns interpretability with system autonomy, enabling AI systems that not only act intelligently but also communicate their reasoning in meaningful and accountable ways.

The proposed application illustrates a practical realisation of LLM-based interpretability within an agentic AI framework. By embedding explanation generation, critique, and reinforcement directly into the system architecture, interpretability becomes a continuous, adaptive, and human-centred process. This design moves beyond traditional post-hoc explanations and demonstrates how interpretability can function as a first-class capability in complex, autonomous AI systems deployed in high-stakes environmental domains.

To support the deployment of LLM-based interpretability within the proposed agentic framework, the system leverages Ollama as the runtime environment for hosting and executing Large Language Models locally [5]. Ollama provides a lightweight and efficient interface for running state-of-the-art LLMs on local infrastructure, abstracting away much of the complexity associated with model loading, optimisation, and inference. This makes it particularly suitable for research-oriented, domain-specific applications where control, transparency, and reproducibility are critical.

From an architectural perspective, Ollama serves as the execution layer for the LLM-powered agents that generate explanations and evaluate them. Rather than relying on external cloud-based APIs, the agentic system communicates directly with locally hosted models via Ollama's API interface. This design choice ensures that explanation generation remains tightly coupled to the system's internal state and messaging flow, allowing agents to exchange structured prompts and receive deterministic, inspectable responses. As a result, interpretability is not outsourced to an opaque external service but remains an integral and observable component of the system.

Ollama supports a variety of open-source LLMs and enables rapid model switching and experimentation without requiring architectural changes at the agent level. This flexibility is particularly important in the context of interpretability, where different models may vary in their reasoning, explanation coherence, or domain adaptation. By decoupling agent logic from the underlying model implementation, the system can evolve its interpretive capabilities while preserving the overall agentic design.

In addition, Ollama's local execution model aligns well with the system's emphasis on grounded, accountable explanations. Since all prompts, responses, and intermediate messages remain within the local execution environment, the full explanation pipeline can be logged, audited, and analysed. This supports transparency not only in what explanations are generated, but also in how they are produced, enabling deeper inspection of agent behaviour and learning dynamics over time.

The use of Ollama also contributes to robustness and data governance, particularly in environmental and scientific domains. Sensitive data, such as location-specific environmental indicators or unpublished observational datasets, do not need to be transmitted to external services for explanation generation. This reduces privacy risks and ensures compliance with data-handling constraints while still enabling advanced natural-language interpretability.

In the proposed framework, the LLM needs to be chosen to generate a response for one agent, while another agent also needs an LLM to evaluate the one that has been created, thereby making it more capable. First, we need to know which models

**Fig. 6.2**  Ollama gemma3 model listing

are available; therefore, Ollama provides a website where one can view all available models. The model chosen is gemma3, as can be seen in Fig. 6.2. It displays various models that differ only in parameter count. As we increase the parameter count, the model is trained on more data and consequently provides better responses, with a deeper knowledge base.

Once the model and parameter count have been chosen, they need to be downloaded to the Ollama repository. This can be achieved by using the terminal with the Ollama environment installed. The available commands are shown in Fig. 6.3, along with their explanations. For our application, we have chosen to use gemma3 with 1 billion parameters for the Response Agent and gemma3 with 27 billion parameters.

To view the downloaded models, use the *ollama list* command, which lists all models with their parameter counts. This is shown in Fig. 6.4, which also shows that gemma3, with 27 billion parameters, has already been downloaded; however, gemma3 with 1 billion parameters is still not available, prompting us to run the necessary download command.

The download can be done by using the correct command. When referring to Fig. 6.3, the command *pull* can be used to download a model from their repository.

```
root@25751351d7ad:/# ollama
Usage:
  ollama [flags]
  ollama [command]

Available Commands:
  serve       Start ollama
  create      Create a model
  show        Show information for a model
  run         Run a model
  stop        Stop a running model
  pull        Pull a model from a registry
  push        Push a model to a registry
  signin      Sign in to ollama.com
  signout     Sign out from ollama.com
  list        List models
  ps          List running models
  cp          Copy a model
  rm          Remove a model
  help        Help about any command

Flags:
  -h, --help      help for ollama
  -v, --version   Show version information

Use "ollama [command] --help" for more information about a command.
```

**Fig. 6.3**  Ollama environment

```
root@25751351d7ad:/# ollama list
NAME                        ID              SIZE      MODIFIED
gpt-oss:20b                 17052f91a42e    13 GB     4 days ago
smollm2:135m                9077fe9d2ae1    270 MB    7 days ago
frob/minimax-m2.1:latest    5ab71149cfc5    138 GB    7 days ago
deepseek-r1:671b            14a4e575643d    404 GB    4 weeks ago
gemma3:27b                  a418f5838eaf    17 GB     4 weeks ago
qwen3:235b                  754a872f1290    142 GB    5 weeks ago
gemma3:4b                   a2af6cc3eb7f    3.3 GB    6 weeks ago
```

**Fig. 6.4**  Ollama downloaded model listing

Therefore, Fig. 6.5 uses this command to download the chosen model and shows the download status. When the success message is displayed, the model variant has been successfully installed.

After the successful installation, the model is now available for use. The Ollama environment provides an Application Programming Interface (API) to use the models remotely. This allows us to separate the modules to run on different equipment, which is much more suitable, as LLMs benefit from using Graphical Processing Units (GPUs) to generate responses much more quickly. Now, to establish a connection to

**Fig. 6.5**  Ollama download of gemma3:1b

ollama, use the URL (e.g., localhost or a specific one if configured), and the default port is 11434. The AutoGen framework allows you to set up an LLM connection, as shown in Listing 6.19. The configuration accepts several parameters, such as *model*, which defines the model to use, available in the Ollama environment. The *base_url* is the URL required to connect to the Ollama API, including the port number. An important note: the URL must end with $/v1$; otherwise, it throws a connection error. The *api_key* is a unique key that authorises the connection; here, Ollama does not expect one, but one was included for consistency. Finally, the *price* allows us to set the price, with the first element the prompt token price and the last the completion price. These parameters are specific to the configuration used to establish the connection; *temperature* is an Ollama environment parameter, where higher values make the model more creative, whereas lower values make it more direct.

```
llm_config_small = {
    "config_list": [
        {
            "model": "gemma3:1b",
            "base_url": "http://MAS_Ollama:11434/v1",
            "api_key": "ollama",
            "price": [0.0001, 0.0001]
        }
    ],
    "temperature": 0.7
}

llm_config_big = {
    "config_list": [
        {
            "model": "gemma3:27b",
            "base_url": "http://MAS_Ollama:11434/v1",
            "api_key": "ollama",
            "price": [0.001, 0.001]
        }
    ],
    "temperature": 0.7
}
```

**Listing 6.19**  AutoGen's LLM Configurations

Prompt 4.1 defines the Response Agent's task: translate a numerical water quality classification into a coherent, human-readable explanation. It instructs the language model to analyse the environmental health of a specific location using the predicted water quality class as contextual grounding, while explicitly acknowledging the space of possible alternative outcomes. By requiring a plain-text response and forbidding code or markdown, the prompt ensures that the generated explanation is accessible to non-technical users. The focus on ecological consequences and probable drivers encourages the model to move beyond mere restatement of the prediction, instead producing a narrative that contextualises the result within environmental processes and observed conditions.

**Prompt 4.1 Response Agent Prompt**

Analyse the environmental health of location (Sao Miguel, Azores) based on its "prediction" water quality rating. Considering the range of possible outcomes (possible_predictions), draft a plain-text paragraph explaining the ecological consequences and the probable drivers behind this prediction. Avoid all code, tables, or markdown in your response.

Prompt 4.2 governs the Test Agent's evaluative behaviour by instructing the language model to critically assess a generated explanation in relation to its originating prompt. The model is asked to score explanation quality on a numerical scale while simultaneously providing a detailed justification for the assigned rating. By explicitly separating reasoning from the final score and enforcing a fixed output format, the prompt yields structured feedback that can be interpreted both qualitatively and quantitatively. This design allows the evaluation output to function as a reward signal for RL, while retaining sufficient explanatory depth to support auditability and human inspection.

**Prompt 4.2 Test Agent Evaluation Prompt**

Perform a critical assessment of the response provided below in relation to its original prompt. Score the quality of the content on a scale of 1 to 10.

Context: Original Prompt: original_prompt Submitted Response: explanation

First, offer a detailed justification for your score. Then, conclude your evaluation by stating the final mark in the format: Rating: x/10.

Prompt 4.3 is used to generate contrastive explanations that serve as reference points for reinforcement-driven learning. Depending on the quality score assigned during evaluation, the language model is instructed either to produce an intentionally poor response or to generate a high-quality alternative to the original explanation. By conditioning response quality on the evaluation outcome, the prompt creates paired examples that explicitly distinguish desirable from undesirable explanatory behaviour. These contrastive samples provide rich supervision for subsequent optimisation, enabling the reinforcement agent to learn not only what constitutes a good explanation but also how poor explanations deviate in relevance, coherence, and fidelity.

> **Prompt 4.3 Test Agent Counter-Response Prompt**
>
> If the reward for the submitted response is high ($> = 7$), produce a response that is intentionally misleading, irrelevant, or of low quality for the original prompt. Otherwise, craft a high-quality, insightful, and comprehensive answer to the prompt.
> Target Prompt: original_prompt
> Deliver only the plain-text response; do not include any code, markdown, or commentary.

Overall, Ollama serves as a critical enabling technology for operationalising LLM-based interpretability within the proposed agentic system. By providing a controllable, flexible, and locally deployable LLM execution environment, it supports the system's broader goals of transparency, adaptability, and continuous improvement. Its integration reinforces the notion that interpretability is not merely a conceptual layer but a concrete, deployable capability embedded within the system's architecture.

## 6.5  Multi-Agent with Reinforcement Learning

The proposed case study realises RL within a multi-agent architecture by distributing learning, evaluation, and optimisation across specialised agents. Rather than embedding RL as a monolithic optimisation process, the framework implements learning as an emergent system-level phenomenon arising from structured interaction between agents with distinct roles. In this architecture, the Test Agent and the Reinforcement Agent form the core evaluative and adaptive loop that enables continuous improvement through Group Relative Policy Optimisation (GRPO).

At the heart of this learning loop is the Test Agent, which evaluates system outputs in a domain-aware, interpretability-focused manner. The Test Agent does not participate in prediction or explanation generation; instead, it operates as an externalised evaluator that assesses the quality of agent outputs relative to predefined criteria. These criteria include predictive consistency, explanatory coherence, domain alignment, and clarity of reasoning. By decoupling evaluation from generation, the architecture preserves objectivity and prevents evaluative bias from contaminating the generative process.

The Test Agent produces evaluative feedback by analysing multiple candidate outputs generated by the explanation-producing agent, specifically the Response Agent. Rather than assigning absolute scalar rewards, the Test Agent performs relative comparisons across outputs. This comparative evaluation reflects the observation that explanation quality is often best judged relationally rather than absolutely. Explanations are ranked, scored, or grouped based on their adherence to domain expectations and interpretability requirements. The resulting evaluative signals capture nuanced distinctions between outputs that would be difficult to encode in fixed reward functions. The Test Agent's output will be used to calculate an evaluation score out of 10, along with a counter-response illustrating what a good or bad response might look like.

These relative evaluations serve as the primary learning signal for the Reinforcement Agent. The Reinforcement Agent is responsible for translating evaluative feedback into policy updates using the GRPO framework. Conceptually, GRPO treats sets of candidate behaviours as a population and optimises policies to increase the likelihood of generating higher-ranked outputs while suppressing less effective ones. In practical terms, this optimisation uses a large language model as the policy for explanation generation. The base model is first loaded in a configuration that prioritises stability and controlled adaptation, as shown in Listing 6.20. Full fine-tuning is explicitly disabled to ensure that learning remains incremental and aligned with prior behaviour distributions.

```
model, tokenizer = FastModel.from_pretrained(
    model_name = model_name,
    max_seq_length = max_seq_length,
    load_in_4bit = False,
    load_in_8bit = False,
    full_finetuning = False,
)
```

**Listing 6.20**  LLM Model Loading

Rather than updating all model parameters, the Reinforcement Agent applies parameter-efficient fine-tuning to selectively adapt the components of the language model most relevant to explanation quality. As illustrated in Listing 6.21, Low-Rank Adaptation modules are introduced into the language, attention, and MultiLayer Perceptron (MLP) layers, while other components remain frozen as for the vision layers, which are not used. This selective adaptation reduces computational overhead and mitigates the risk of destabilising the model while still allowing the policy to respond meaningfully to evaluative feedback from the Test Agent.

```
1  model = FastModel.get_peft_model(
2      model,
3      finetune_vision_layers = False,
4      finetune_language_layers = True,
5      finetune_attention_modules = True,
6      finetune_mlp_modules = True,
7
8      r = 8,
9      lora_alpha = 8,
10     lora_dropout = 0,
11     bias = "none",
12     random_state = 3407,
13 )
```

**Listing 6.21** PEFT LLM Model Retrieval

The configuration shown in Listing 6.22 governs how evaluative feedback from the Test Agent is transformed into stable policy updates within the GRPO framework. The learning rate is set conservatively to $5e-6$ to ensure that updates induced by relative ranking signals remain incremental. This is particularly important in preference-based optimisation, where reward signals are comparative rather than absolute and can exhibit higher variance. The Adam optimisation parameters ($adam\_beta1$ and $adam\_beta2$) are tuned to balance responsiveness to new evaluative feedback with smoothing across optimisation steps, while $weight\_decay$ introduces regularisation that discourages overfitting to short-term evaluative preferences.

The warm-up strategy ($warmup\_ratio$) and cosine learning rate scheduler are used to stabilise early training dynamics, allowing the policy to adapt gradually as group-level feedback becomes available. This is especially relevant in GRPO, where optimisation operates over distributions of candidate outputs rather than single trajectories. The choice of a fused AdamW optimiser further supports numerical stability and efficient convergence during iterative policy updates.

Batch size and gradient accumulation are deliberately set to one, reflecting the structure of the learning signal rather than hardware limitations. In this setting, each optimisation step corresponds to a small group of generated explanations associated with a single prompt, preserving the semantic coherence of group-level comparisons. The $num_generations$ parameter explicitly controls the number of candidate explanations sampled per prompt, forming the population over which relative ranking and reward normalisation are performed. This parameter is central to GRPO, as it defines the resolution at which comparative evaluation occurs and directly influences the diversityâŁ"quality trade-off in candidate outputs.

The parameters $max\_prompt\_length$ and $max\_completion\_length$ constrain the model's inputâŁ"output interface, ensuring that optimisation focuses on explanatory content rather than prompt formatting artefacts. By bounding the completion length relative to the maximum sequence length, the configuration enforces consistency across generations, simplifying comparative evaluation by the Test Agent.

Training duration is controlled by $max\_steps$ rather than epochs, reflecting the continuous, asynchronous nature of learning in the multi-agent setting. Model checkpoints are saved at fixed step intervals, enabling inspection of policy evolution without interrupting the learning loop. Gradient norm clipping (*max_grad_norm*) provides an additional stabilisation mechanism, preventing large updates that could arise from outlier evaluations or highly skewed rankings within a group.

```
training_args = GRPOConfig(
    learning_rate = 5e-6,
    adam_beta1 = 0.9,
    adam_beta2 = 0.99,
    weight_decay = 0.1,
    warmup_ratio = 0.1,
    lr_scheduler_type = "cosine",
    optim = "adamw_torch_fused",
    logging_steps = 1,
    per_device_train_batch_size = 1,
    gradient_accumulation_steps = 1,
    num_generations = 4,
    max_prompt_length = max_prompt_length,
    max_completion_length = max_seq_length - max_prompt_length,
    max_steps = 50,
    save_steps = 50,
    max_grad_norm = 0.1,
    report_to = "none",
    output_dir = "outputs",
)
```

**Listing 6.22**  GRPO Configuration

The learning loop is completed by instantiating a GRPO trainer that binds together the adapted model, the evaluation-derived reward function, and the dataset constructed from logged agent interactions. As shown in Listing 6.23, the reward function encodes the relative assessments produced by the Test Agent, allowing the Reinforcement Agent to update the policy based on comparative quality signals rather than absolute task outcomes. This closes the evaluative loop between generation, assessment, and optimisation.

```
trainer = GRPOTrainer(
    model = model,
    processing_class = tokeniser,
    args = training_args,
    train_dataset = dataset,
    reward_funcs = [reward_func]
)
```

**Listing 6.23**  GRPO Trainer Initialisation

The Reinforcement Agent maintains a controlled learning dynamic by constraining policy updates to remain close to prior behaviour distributions. This stabilisation principle, inherited from earlier policy optimisation methods, ensures that improvements are incremental and prevents abrupt shifts that could degrade performance or produce incoherent explanations. GRPO extends this stabilisation to group-level evaluation, enabling learning to occur across output distributions rather than on a single trajectory.

Communication between the Test Agent and the Reinforcement Agent is mediated through structured messages that encode evaluation results, rankings, and contextual metadata. These messages do not expose raw model internals but provide sufficient information for learning to proceed in a grounded and auditable manner. This design supports transparency in the learning process, allowing evaluative decisions and their influence on learning to be independently inspected.

Importantly, the learning loop operates asynchronously with respect to generation and deployment. Explanations can be generated and delivered while evaluation and reinforcement occur in parallel or in subsequent cycles. This temporal decoupling enables the system to operate continuously without requiring synchronised retraining phases. From a learning dynamics perspective, this structure introduces delayed reinforcement, in which policy updates reflect aggregated evaluative feedback across multiple interaction episodes.

The multi-agent RL framework also supports modular extensibility. Additional evaluative agents can be introduced to assess alternative dimensions, such as fairness, uncertainty communication, or regulatory compliance. Their feedback can be integrated into the GRPO process either as additional comparative dimensions or as constraints on acceptable policy updates. This modularity reflects an agentic design philosophy in which learning objectives can evolve without requiring a redesign of the core architecture.

At the system level, learning emerges from the interaction between generation, evaluation, and optimisation rather than from any single agent. The Test Agent does not learn in the traditional sense; rather, it shapes the learning landscape through its evaluations. The Reinforcement Agent does not directly observe task outcomes but infers improvement directions through relative feedback. Together, they form a closed evaluative loop that aligns system behaviour with domain-specific interpretability objectives.

This architecture illustrates how RL can be embedded within agentic systems as a distributed, interpretable, and controllable process. By externalising evaluation and grounding optimisation in relative comparisons, the framework mitigates common challenges in RL for abstract domains, such as reward misspecification and instability. The use of GRPO enables the system to refine the quality of explanations over time while preserving stability, transparency, and alignment with domain expectations.

In summary, the case study demonstrates a concrete instantiation of multi-agent RL in which learning is not confined to a single policy or model but emerges from coordinated interaction between specialised agents. The Test Agent and Reinforcement Agent jointly operationalise GRPO as a system-level learning mechanism, providing a principled pathway for continuous, domain-aware optimisation within an agentic AI framework.

# References


1. Tymoteusz Miller et al. "Integrating Artificial Intelligence Agents with the Internet of Things for Enhanced Environmental Monitoring: Applications in Water Quality and Climate Data". In: *Electronics* 14.4 (2025). ISSN: 2079-9292. DOI: 10.3390/electronics14040696.
2. Niloufar Alipour Talemi, Julia Boone, and Fatemeh Afghah. *Agentic AI in Remote Sensing: Foundations, Taxonomy, and Emerging Systems*. 2026. DOI: 10.48550/arXiv.2601.01891. arXiv: 2601.01891 [cs.CV].
3. Yu Li, Feng Han, and Yi Zheng. "Artificial Intelligence in Surface Water Quality Research and Management: Recent Progress and Future Directions". In: *Ecosystem Health and Sustainability* (2026). DOI: 10.34133/ehs.0474.
4. Rafael Barbarroxa et al. "Benchmarking AutoGen with different large language models". In: *IEEE Conference on Artificial Intelligence (CAI)*. 2024, pp. 263–264. DOI: 10.1109/CAI59869.2024.00058.
5. Francisco S. Marcondes et al. *Natural Language Analytics with Generative Large-Language Models: A Practical Approach with Ollama and Open-Source LLMs*. Springer Cham, 2025. DOI: 10.1007/978-3-031-76631-2.
6. Feibo Jiang et al. "From large ai models to agentic ai: A tutorial on future intelligent communications". In: *arXiv preprint* arXiv:2505.22311 (2025). DOI: 10.48550/arXiv.2505.22311.
7. Deepak Bhaskar Acharya, Karthigeyan Kuppan, and B. Divya. "Agentic AI: Autonomous Intelligence for Complex Goals—A Comprehensive Survey". In: *IEEE Access* 13 (2025), pp. 18912–18936. DOI: 10.1109/ACCESS.2025.3532853.
8. Adrián Regos et al. "Mainstreaming remotely sensed ecosystem functioning in ecological niche models". In: *Remote Sensing in Ecology and Conservation* 8.4 (2022), pp. 431–447. DOI: 10.1002/rse2.255.
9. Wayne Xin Zhao et al. "A survey of large language models". In: *arXiv preprint* arXiv:2303.18223 1.2 (2023). DOI: 10.1145/3744746.
10. Junfeng Jiao et al. "Navigating llm ethics: Advancements, challenges, and future directions". In: *AI and Ethics* (2025), pp. 1–25. DOI: 10.1007/s43681-025-00814-5.
11. Ajay Bandi et al. "The Rise of Agentic AI: A Review of Definitions, Frameworks, Architectures, Applications, Evaluation Metrics, and Challenges". In: *Future Internet* 17.9 (2025). ISSN: 1999-5903. DOI: 10.3390/fi17090404.
12. Devis Tuia et al. "Artificial Intelligence to Advance Earth Observation: A review of models, recent trends, and pathways forward". In: *IEEE Geoscience and Remote Sensing Magazine* 13.4 (Dec. 2025), pp. 119–141. ISSN: 2473-2397. DOI: 10.1109/mgrs.2024.3425961.
13. Christoph Schröer, Felix Kruse, and Jorge Marx Gómez. "A Systematic Literature Review on Applying CRISP-DM Process Model". In: *Procedia Computer Science* 181 (2021). CENTERIS 2020 - International Conference on ENTERprise Information Systems / ProjMAN 2020 - International Conference on Project MANagement / HCist 2020 - International Conference on Health and Social Care Information Systems and Technologies 2020, CENTERIS/ProjMAN/HCist 2020, pp. 526–534. ISSN: 1877-0509. DOI: 10.1016/j.procs.2021.01.199.

# Chapter 7
# Conclusion

**Abstract** For those who thought Artificial Intelligence (AI) was limited to cold calculations, this work's conclusion reveals a horizon where machines learn to deliberate with purpose and ethics. AI has ceased to be a set of static prediction algorithms and has transformed into dynamic systems of action and reaction. The core of this evolution lies in the transition from simple technical autonomy to cognitive agents, allowing systems to possess internal representations of objectives and contexts. The proposed technical infrastructure, which integrates Multi-Agent Systems (MAS), Reinforcement Learning (RL), and Large Language Models (LLMs), enables social coordination, experience-driven plasticity, and semantic mediation. The case study in the Azores lakes validated the practice, demonstrating that task decomposition using Cross-Industry Standard Process for Data Mining (CRISP-DM) and 'artificial deliberation' in GroupChat leads to consistent decisions. The use of the Group Relative Policy Optimisation (GRPO) algorithm and the local Ollama platform ensures policy stability and data sovereignty. By treating interpretability as an intrinsic design requirement, agentic architectures guarantee transparency and human trust. The future holds challenges in scaling semantic coordination and artificial metacognition, aiming for a symbiosis in which technology serves the common good.

## 7.1  Summary of Key Contributions

To understand the relevance of the advances discussed in this book, it is necessary to situate the contributions within the discipline's historical evolution. AI has ceased to be seen merely as a set of static prediction algorithms and has become a dynamic system of action and reaction. The fundamental contribution of this work lies in the formalisation of a framework that enables artificial systems not only to 'think' about data but also to act upon it with a sense of purpose. This formalisation is essential to address the challenges of complexity and uncertainty that characterise contemporary real-world environments.

From this perspective, the distinction between conventional technical autonomy and cognitive agency constitutes one of the most solid foundations established in


P. Oliveira et al., *Architectures for Agentic AI*, SpringerBriefs in Intelligent Systems,
https://doi.org/10.1007/978-3-032-24781-0_7

this book. It has been demonstrated that, while autonomy focuses on the independent execution of predefined tasks, Agentic AI requires functional intentionality, in which the system possesses an internal representation of its objectives and the context of its actions. This shift in focus has allowed us to recognise the need for architectures that support mechanisms for strategic deliberation and behavioural adaptation, ensuring that the system knows not only what to do but also why it is acting in response to environmental changes.

The integration of MAS, RL, and LLMs emerges as the essential technical infrastructure for this new generation of intelligence. This book has demonstrated that these three domains, previously treated in isolation, are the axes that enable social coordination, experience-driven plasticity, and semantic mediation through Natural Language Processing (NLP). The ability of a system to act collectively, learn from the consequences of its decisions, and explain its reasoning in human terms is what defines the level of agentic intelligence proposed here.

The critical analysis of orchestration architectures–such as LangChain, AutoGen, and CrewAI–allowed us to map the design space available for building agentic systems [1]. We identified that a system's effectiveness depends on the balance between deterministic control and the emergence of cooperative behaviours [2]. By detailing how these tools manage autonomy and communication, this book offers a guide to selecting the most appropriate orchestration framework for each problem, whether through controlled execution chains or decentralised dialogues managed by coordinating agents.

Another important milestone of this book is establishing language-based interpretability as an intrinsic design requirement. Instead of treating explanation as an optional feature or a process separate from decision-making, the architectures presented here integrate explanatory capability directly into the reasoning cycle [3]. The use of LLMs to translate internal states and complex interactions into understandable narratives is fundamental to ensuring transparency and auditability, allowing systems not only to operate autonomously but also to remain under the aegis of human understanding and trust [4].

Finally, the exploration of learning dynamics, focusing on the transition from methods such as Proximal Policy Optimisation (PPO) to GRPO, highlighted the importance of alignment based on comparative evaluations. This book has proven that, in complex and subjective domains, learning is more stable when guided by group feedback and reflective critiques from evaluating agents. This reinforcement approach not only improves task effectiveness but also refines the quality of the explanations generated, closing the loop between technical action and the social communication of agentic intelligence.

## 7.2 Insights Into Autonomous Decision-Making

The transition from theoretical foundations to practical implementation yielded valuable insights into the nature of autonomous decision-making in real-world ecosystems [5]. Through a case study focused on monitoring the Azorean lakes, it was observed that applying agentic theories requires greater sensitivity to integrating heterogeneous data sources. The environmental complexity of them served as an ideal testing ground to demonstrate that distributed intelligence can overcome the limitations of static predictive models by transforming satellite data and chemical parameters into narratives to support decision-making [6].

One of the most profound reflections from the practice was the effectiveness of functional task decomposition into specialised agents, as outlined in the CRISP-DM methodology [7]. By structuring the system into layers of acquisition, preparation, prediction, explanation, and evaluation, the book demonstrated that modularity is not just an engineering choice but an imperative for the robustness of autonomous systems [8]. This separation allowed each agent to operate with clear local objectives, while collective intelligence emerged from coordinated interaction, demonstrating that the complexity of an environmental problem can be managed through harmonised micro-decisions within a common dialogue space.

The management of real-time conversational orchestration demonstrated that dialogue between agents is a more flexible coordination mechanism than rigid execution sequences. In the AutoGen environment, agents' ability to observe shared context in GroupChat and adjust their responses based on peer feedback enabled a form of 'artificial deliberation' that mimics human consultation processes [9]. This dynamic was crucial to ensure that the classification of water quality and its subsequent explanation were consistent with the biological parameters and ethical constraints imposed on the system.

The practice also highlighted the vital role of RL in stabilising multi-agent systems affected by non-stationarity [10]. During the system's development, it was observed that the learning of one agent influenced the operating conditions of the others, creating a dynamic and unstable environment. The implementation of the GRPO algorithm, mediated by an independent evaluation agent (Test Agent), enabled the system to stabilise its communication policies via relative reward signals, demonstrating that autonomous self-improvement is viable when a rigorous cycle of internal critique and review is established.

Another fundamental insight concerned the importance of local execution infrastructure for data sovereignty and decision agility. The use of Ollama to manage models like Gemma3 allowed the system to operate quickly and securely, without relying on external communications to generate explanations or evaluations [11]. This infrastructural autonomy proved essential in sensitive domains where environmental data privacy and service continuity are paramount, reinforcing the idea that agentic intelligence must be deeply anchored in the physical and technological environment in which it operates.

Finally, the experience of translating theory into practice revealed that transparency is the most significant catalyst for human decision-makers to adopt these technologies. The system did not limit itself to issuing classifications; it generated internal symbolic discussions that resulted in accessible linguistic justifications. This ability to transform technical analysis into an intelligible interdisciplinary reasoning process is what allows AI to act not only as a tool, but as a true partner in the sustainable management of our natural heritage.

## 7.3  Wider Impact and Significance

The impact of this book extends far beyond the boundaries of information technology, influencing how we conceive of collaboration between humanity and technology in the 21st century [12]. By laying the groundwork for an agentic AI that is both proactive and explainable, we contribute to a profound shift in the role of artificial systems in society. We move away from seeing them as black boxes of automation and towards considering them active employees who participate in discovery, analysis, and decision-making processes, expanding the horizon of our own collective cognition.

The scientific significance of this work lies in proposing an intelligence centred on process and relationship, rather than solely on statistical results. By integrating perception, communication, and learning into a reflective circuit, the agentic architectures proposed here offer a model of distributed rationality that is resilient to uncertainty. This paradigm is particularly relevant for addressing global crises, such as climate change and natural resource management, where the ability to monitor, interpret, and act in a coordinated manner is essential for ecological and social resilience.

From an ethical and governance perspective, the focus on interpretability and normative alignment addresses critical challenges of transparency and accountability [13]. A system capable of justifying its decisions in NLP and of adjusting its behaviour in accordance with ethical and biological principles enables more effective and democratic human oversight. This accountability is fundamental to ensuring that agents' autonomy does not compromise the security and values of human societies, promoting a technology that is, by design, responsible and transparent [14].

The democratisation of scientific knowledge is another transformative consequence of agentic intelligence. Through the linguistic mediation of LLMs, complex technical data and opaque model predictions are translated into intelligible narratives for experts in diverse fields and the general public. This societal impact is vital to ensuring that advances in machine autonomy do not create new forms of exclusion but serve as bridges of understanding that facilitate the participatory management of territory and the environment.

Furthermore, this book highlights the concept of 'artificial cognitive ecosystems' in which intelligence emerges not from isolated processing but from a network of continuous interactions, learning, and communication. This vision has a lasting impact on how we design digital infrastructures, moving from centralised, rigid systems to flexible, adaptable agent networks. The significance of this shift lies in the robustness and scalability that these architectures confer on public services, logistics, and digital governance in an increasingly interconnected world.

In short, by endowing machines with reasoning, we are not only making them more efficient; we are making them meaningful participants in our shared world. The long-term impact of this book will be measured by our ability to integrate these cognitive partners harmoniously into our reality, ensuring that technology serves as a powerful ally for a deeper understanding and sustainable preservation of the planet.

## 7.4  Future Research Directions

Despite the significant progress detailed here, the field of Agentic AI is at an evolutionary stage that opens numerous windows for future research. One of the primary challenges relates to the scalability of semantic coordination in large-scale systems [15]. As the number of agents and the density of communications grow, the risk of cognitive fragmentation and information overload increases proportionally [16]. Investigating how to manage dialogue hierarchies and information synthesis mechanisms that preserve global coherence without sacrificing local agility will be a vital area of study in the coming years.

The robustness and reliability of NLP-generated explanations constitute another critical research vector. Although this book has proposed peer-review and reinforcement-learning alignment mechanisms, the problem of 'explanation hallucination' in LLMs demands deeper solutions. The development of methods that deterministically link linguistic justifications to verifiable perception data and agent execution logics will be fundamental to raising technical confidence to absolute levels in highly critical domains.

Exploring artificial metacognition architectures and systemic reflexivity represents an essential step towards more resilient autonomy. Equipping agents with the ability to monitor not only the environment but also their own knowledge limits, reasoning processes, and deliberative uncertainty will allow systems to detect inconsistencies and proactively adjust their strategies. Investigating how these second-order capabilities can be formalised and integrated into continuous learning cycles will be crucial for the long-term stability of agentic systems.

Another promising research direction lies in the development of agentic communication languages that combine the flexibility of NLP with the precision of symbolic formal models. Studying how agents can learn communication protocols that are both efficient for machine cooperation and transparent to human understanding will pave the way for more integrated collective intelligence ecosystems. Research into the transfer of learned knowledge and policies across heterogeneous domains will also be crucial for reducing implementation costs in new application areas.

Security and defence against adversarial behaviour in decentralised agentic systems will require extra attention. Ensuring that social coordination and reinforcement learning remain resilient to manipulation or uncooperative agents is imperative for deploying agentic networks in vital infrastructure. The development of technical trust protocols based on cryptographic proofs and real-time auditing of agentic messages and decisions will constitute a fundamental pillar of future cybersecurity.

Finally, research should focus on the symbiosis between AI and human wisdom in shared decision-making cycles. Exploring how agentic systems can be designed to act as cognitive 'coaches' or mediators in complex human deliberation processes will transform how we resolve conflicts and manage the common good. The future of this book is not an endpoint, but an invitation to explore a horizon where technology and humanity co-evolve in harmony, guided by responsibility and mutual understanding.

## 7.5   Final Remarks

Upon concluding this book, it becomes evident that the trajectory of AI, from its symbolic origins to its current agentic state, represents an unprecedented movement of integration and sophistication. The transition from machine to agent, from static calculation to dynamic deliberation, and from isolated prediction to coordinated understanding, is not merely a technological advancement but a reconfiguration of our own relationship with knowledge and action. Intelligence has ceased to be merely a property of processing and has become a property of situated interaction in the world.

The architectures for Agentic AI discussed and operationalised here through the Azores case study demonstrate that it is possible to build systems that participate meaningfully and transparently in solving complex problems. By uniting social coordination, learning plasticity, and linguistic mediation, we offer science and society a new grammar for intelligent action, in which technology serves as a proactive ally in the preservation and understanding of our planet.

This book concludes with the conviction that Agentic AI constitutes the fundamental pillar for the next generation of decision-making systems. The ability of machines to continuously learn from experience and communicate their reasoning intelligibly is what will allow us to build a lasting relationship of trust between society and AI. The future lies in this symbiosis, where technological autonomy is guided by human responsibility and an ethical commitment to the common good.

Ultimately, what we define as agentic intelligence is the promise of a technology that not only processes information but also inhabits and cares for the context in which it is embedded. By transforming passive monitoring into active deliberation, this paradigm equips us to address the most pressing global challenges with clarity and determination. May this work serve as a foundation for future explorations, inspiring the development of systems that honour the world's complexity and human dignity.

The journey from calculation to deliberation described here is only the beginning of a new stage in our technological history. As agentic systems become more integrated into our lives, our own capacity for understanding will be expanded by these cognitive partners. The final invitation is for us to continue building this future with boldness and caution, ensuring that AI remains an instrument of enlightenment and progress for all humanity.

# References


1. Shuang Ying Chin and Dr Ng Kok Why. "Comparative of Multi-Agent System Frameworks: Crewai, Langchain, and Autogen". In: *Langchain, and Autogen* (2024). DOI: https://doi.org/10.2139/ssrn.5367964.
2. Jianrui Wang et al. "Cooperative and Competitive Multi-Agent Systems: From Optimization to Games". In: *IEEE/CAA Journal of Automatica Sinica* 9.5 (2022), pp. 763–783. DOI: https://doi.org/10.1109/JAS.2022.105506.
3. Jingyuan Yang et al. "Enhancing Semantic Consistency of Large Language Models through Model Editing: An Interpretability-Oriented Approach". In: *Findings of the Association for Computational Linguistics: ACL 2024*. Ed. by Lun-Wei Ku, Andre Martins, and Vivek Srikumar. Bangkok, Thailand: Association for Computational Linguistics, Aug. 2024, pp. 3343–3353. DOI: https://doi.org/10.18653/v1/2024.findings-acl.199.
4. Cheonsu Jeong. "Design and Evaluation Methods for LLM-Based Explainable AI (XAI)-Based Human-AI Collaboration Systems". In: *Advances in Artificial Intelligence and Machine Learning* 5.3 (2025), p. 240. DOI: https://doi.org/10.54364/AAIML.2025.53240.
5. Niloufar Alipour Talemi, Julia Boone, and Fatemeh Afghah. *Agentic AI in Remote Sensing: Foundations, Taxonomy, and Emerging Systems*. 2026. DOI: https://doi.org/10.48550/arXiv.2601.01891. arXiv: 2601.01891 [cs.CV].
6. Adrián Regos et al. "Mainstreaming remotely sensed ecosystem functioning in ecological niche models". In: *Remote Sensing in Ecology and Conservation* 8.4 (2022), pp. 431–447. DOI: https://doi.org/10.1002/rse2.255.
7. Christoph Schröer, Felix Kruse, and Jorge Marx Gómez. "A Systematic Literature Review on Applying CRISP-DM Process Model". In: *Procedia Computer Science* 181 (2021). CENTERIS 2020 - International Conference on ENTERprise Information Systems / ProjMAN 2020 - International Conference on Project MANagement / HCist 2020 - International Conference on Health and Social Care Information Systems and Technologies 2020, CENTERIS/ProjMAN/HCist 2020, pp. 526–534. ISSN: 1877-0509. DOI: https://doi.org/10.1016/j.procs.2021.01.199.
8. Rob H. Bemthuis, Ruben R. Govers, and Amin Asadi. "A CRISP-DM-based methodology for assessing agent-based simulation models using process mining". In: *Journal of Simulation* 0.0 (2025), pp. 1–22. DOI: https://doi.org/10.1080/17477778.2025.2508245.
9. Qingyun Wu et al. *AutoGen: Enabling Next-Gen LLM Applications via Multi-Agent Conversation*. 2023. DOI: https://doi.org/10.48550/arXiv.2308.08155. arXiv: 2308.08155 [cs.AI].
10. Hadi Nekoei et al. "Dealing With Non-stationarity in Decentralized Cooperative Multi-Agent Deep Reinforcement Learning via Multi-Timescale Learning". In: *Proceedings of The 2nd Conference on Lifelong Learning Agents*. Ed. by Sarath Chandar et al. Vol. 232. Proceedings of Machine Learning Research. PMLR, 2023, pp. 376–398. DOI: https://doi.org/10.48550/arXiv.2302.02792.
11. Francisco S. Marcondes et al. *Natural Language Analytics with Generative Large-Language Models: A Practical Approach with Ollama and Open-Source LLMs*. Springer Cham, 2025. DOI: https://doi.org/10.1007/978-3-031-76631-2.
12. Pierpaolo Magliocca et al. "Understanding human–technology interaction: evolving boundaries". In: *European Journal of Innovation Management* 28.5 (Oct. 2024), pp. 2006–2028. ISSN: 1460-1060. DOI: https://doi.org/10.1108/EJIM-04-2024-0341.

13.  Ben Chester Cheong. "Transparency and accountability in AI systems: safeguarding wellbeing in the age of algorithmic decision-making". In: *Frontiers in Human Dynamics* Volume 6 - 2024 (2024). ISSN: 2673-2726. DOI: https://doi.org/10.3389/fhumd.2024.1421273.

14.  Junfeng Jiao et al. "Navigating llm ethics: Advancements, challenges, and future directions". In: *AI and Ethics* (2025), pp. 1–25. DOI: https://doi.org/10.1007/s43681-025-00814-5.

15.  Zain Asgar, Michelle Nguyen, and Sachin Katti. *Efficient and Scalable Agentic AI with Heterogeneous Systems*. 2025. DOI: https://doi.org/10.48550/arXiv.2507.19635. arXiv: 2507.19635 [cs.LG].

16.  Sarfraz Brohi et al. "A Research Landscape of Agentic AI and Large Language Models: Applications, Challenges and Future Directions". In: *Algorithms* 18.8 (2025). ISSN: 1999-4893. DOI: https://doi.org/10.3390/a18080499.

GPSR Compliance

The European Union's (EU) General Product Safety Regulation (GPSR) is a set of rules that requires consumer products to be safe and our obligations to ensure this.

If you have any concerns about our products, you can contact us on

ProductSafety@springernature.com

In case Publisher is established outside the EU, the EU authorized representative is:

Springer Nature Customer Service Center GmbH
Europaplatz 3
69115 Heidelberg, Germany